B+T '26

$26.

SHOOT
THE
WIDOW

SHOOT THE WIDOW

Adventures of a Biographer in Search of Her Subject

MERYLE SECREST

ALFRED A. KNOPF   NEW YORK   2007

THIS IS A BORZOI BOOK
PUBLISHED BY ALFRED A. KNOPF

Copyright © 2007 by Meryle Secrest Beveridge

Library of Congress Cataloging-in-Publication Data
Secrest, Meryle.
Shoot the widow : adventures of a biographer in search of
her subject / Meryle Secrest.
—1st ed.
p. cm.
ISBN 978-0-307-26483-1
1. Secrest, Meryle.   2. Biographers—United States—
Biography.   3. Women biographers—United States—
Biography.   4. Washington (D.C.)—Biography.
5. Bath (England)—Biography.   I. Title.
CT275.S4268A3 2007
920.72—dc22
[B]   2006048868

Manufactured in the United States of America
First Edition

For my husband,

who taught me to find the fun in sometimes
unfunny situations,

and for

Uncle Reggie, Reginald Doman,
who knew that already

The first rule of biography: shoot the widow.

—*Justin Kaplan*

Contents

Illustrations

Illustrations are courtesy of the author unless otherwise credited.

Illustrations

SHOOT
THE
WIDOW

Chapter One

The Glass Pavilion

Before I became a biographer I used to write interviews for the *Washington Post* and one day I was sent along to interview Kenneth Clark. The British art historian, who was also a celebrated lecturer, author, university professor, gallery director, patron, collector, social lion and courtier, was at the height of his fame as star of the television series *Civilisation*. A wide international audience had, as it were, fallen in love with him. Roses were practically being thrown at his feet and further accolades would follow his disarming, self-revelatory memoir, *Another Part of the Wood*.

I found him in Georgetown at the home of the founding director of the National Gallery of Art. David Finley was, by then, a small, shrunken and noncommittal figure who, I would belatedly discover, had locked away forever secrets of the art world acquired during a lifetime of firsthand observation. It was 1969. Clark entered the room as if he had stepped out of a picture frame, looking exactly right. He was in his sixties and still handsome, with even features, a beautifully shaped head and an expansive brow. The amiably goofy Bertie Wooster, hero of P. G. Wodehouse's comedies, who employs the frighteningly erudite Jeeves, was wont to explain that his butler's brainpower came

"Roses thrown at his feet": Kenneth Clark in *Civilisation*

from eating fish and the way his head stuck out at the back. As I recall, Kenneth Clark preferred lamb or roast beef and Yorkshire pudding to fish, and the only thing that ever stuck out at the back was his hair. For me, the essence of penetrating intelligence is exemplified by the forehead, and his was as serene and sweeping as any I had seen. I took particular note of what the British would call his keen gaze, so full of energy and expression, and the way he caressed one of his host's delicate alabaster *objets*. There was something curiously familiar about him. But the fact that I had just viewed all thirteen episodes of *Civilisation* must explain why I seemed able to predict his movements, gestures and shades of expression.

Before Clark became a television performer and "national icon," as David Cannadine called him, he had been Keeper of Fine Art at the Ashmolean, director of London's National Gallery, Slade Professor of Fine Art at Oxford, chairman of the Arts Council and Independent Television Authority, as well as the author of books on art and artists, including works on Leonardo da Vinci, Rembrandt, Piero della Francesca, and *The Nude*. He talked freely and fluently and, after I sent him the article, wrote to thank me. This seemed to call for a magazine piece. I persuaded *Smithsonian* magazine to let me interview him again, which wasn't too difficult. The following summer I flew to England to visit the Clarks in their castle outside Hythe in Kent.

It was a Saturday morning, and Lord Clark met me at the station. Lady Clark—Jane—was having her hair done. We would pick her up and then go to Saltwood Castle for lunch. I had dressed for the occasion in my latest affectation, what James Laver would have called a Robin Hood outfit, complete with tunic and matching pants. My host met me in Scottish tweeds, a green velour hat and matching suede shoes. (Jeeves would have taken a very dim view of the shoes.) I could not have looked any more out of place if I had been carrying a bow and arrow, but Lord Clark, his manners as always faultless, rose above it.

There was a heavy summer rain, and as the wait might be prolonged we went for a quick one. Kenneth Clark pulled the Wolsey right up to the front steps of Folkestone's largest hotel, but not before I had surreptitiously taken note of the ten-year-old car's low mileage (6,000) and the two books inside the glove compartment: *Charles Darwin and His World* and *The Odes of Pindar*. "This is what my father used to call a beezer," he said as we dashed inside. When he said a quick one, he meant it. He downed his whiskies rather the way Russians toss back vodka; now you see it, now you don't. I had barely started on a martini when it was time to squelch back down the steps to the car with its dashing red interior. He had left the window open on his side. "Oh well," he said, "I shall get a wet bottom," and we drove off.

He was the second Kenneth Mackenzie Clark. The first was an immensely wealthy Scot, one of the Clarks of Paisley who made their fortunes in the manufacture of sewing thread, and

"The piquant, pouting look": Jane Clark

his father had acquired more than £1 million when he sold his share of the business in 1896. That made him very rich indeed, with all sorts of fashionable addresses, but what always interested me was that he called himself "K." My subject, therefore, always called himself "K," and the complexities of that identification and its implications for his artistic and emotional heritage kept me awake at night in years to come. For the moment I was dazzled enough to be told, after addressing him as Lord Clark, "My friends always call me 'K.' "

K and I drew up at Miss Dora Clifford's hair salon, and Lady Clark edged into the back seat. I had seen pictures of her in her twenties, with a boyish cut, an embroidered stole flung negligently over one shoulder. It was a bit disappointing to find her wearing an entirely conventional tweed suit, her single fashion statement a pair of knit hose with a lacy pattern up the front that drew discreet attention to a shapely pair of legs. Her face seemed wider and softer. There was no trace of the piquant, almost

"It was a real castle": Saltwood

pouting look of the early photographs. It was hard to imagine her as the bold, assertive Jane who had told her friends, in 1953, "We've taken a castle in Kent!" That, Diana Menuhin thought, begged for Beatrice Lillie's retort, "Put it back at once!" Her husband led the conversation, which formed an abbreviated travelogue as we traversed Folkestone's slick and deserted front. She spoke about the well-publicized breakup between Laurence Olivier and Vivien Leigh, whom they knew well, with a tantalizing comment that she did not pursue. In fact, much of her conversation had an oddly disjointed quality, but I attributed that to her husband's flow of confident comments.

It was a real castle, as romantic as anything imagined by Walter Scott. Considered one of the finest examples of a small Norman fortress in England, its turrets and battlements were picturesquely arranged around a partial moat, with an expanse of faultless green lawn on the opposite side and great masses of roses climbing over broken walls. One building that now housed Lord Clark's library was the Archbishop's audience hall where, legend had it, the four knights of Henry II had planned to murder Thomas à Becket. Saltwood even had a ghost story of sorts; several guests, including the actress Irene Worth, had heard voices in the yellow bedroom and the sound of bells at five in the morning. Kenneth Clark had heard them himself. My own response to a building of such splendor and antiquity was mixed. I had a confused impression of stone halls, stained-glass windows, arches, huge fireplaces, silk velvet upholstery, daisies in vases, oils, watercolors and drawings by Henry Moore, Graham Sutherland and Cézanne. Yet there was something austere, if not forbidding, about the atmosphere that the use of inviting fabrics, flowers, down cushions, tapestries and Persian carpets could not dispel. Kenneth Clark said they were building a house on one floor because, he continued, with a gesture toward an ominously long flight of stone steps, Jane tended to "tumble about a bit." It appeared she had fallen down this flight and broken an arm; I was surprised she had not killed herself. His description of the event seemed so offhand as to be jolting.

Lunch was almost ready, organized by K, who seemed in charge of everything. There was just about time for one of his terrifyingly abbreviated cocktail hours. I got another martini. Jane asked for the same, but was not given one. As we sat down to lunch, she remonstrated weakly, "K, you forgot my martini." He was obviously pretending not to hear. We had lamb on Chinese porcelain, with mint sauce in a silver bowl. There were raspberries and cream for dessert; it was perfection. K opened an excellent white Bordeaux, and he and I polished it off between us. Jane Clark had, at most, half a glass. Then the most amazing thing happened. Like the Cheshire cat, she was vanishing before our eyes. Almost the only thing left was the smile as she, on silent feet, glided off to bed. I would learn that she was a famous drunk, said to have fallen down in more embassies than any other woman in England. She seemed almost grateful for the idea that K was going to show me around the castle grounds, and at her suggestion we made our way to the scullery, where I was fitted out with a pair of wellies. Some time after that we ended our tour in K's study, on either side of a fireplace. In my muddy boots and principal boy pantomime outfit I hardly qualified as a femme fatale. So I was astounded to be pulled to my feet by K, who then wrapped me in his arms and said something outlandish like having loved me from the moment he saw me. I was quite grateful to be deposited, soon afterwards, on the train back to London—something like the 4:15.

In his youth, Kenneth Clark had been a runner, and when I got to know him he was still running. It would not be too much of an overstatement to say that he could shoot out of bed, take his morning tea, bathe, be dressed and ready for action in the time it took the rest of us to stagger to the front door for the morning paper. His opening gambit when he met you at the station on the 12:10 would be an enthusiastic description of a fast train back to London at 1:50 p.m. "He terrifies me when he is in this mood," one of his girlfriends, Margaret Slythe, said. "He's like a train shunting us through the station." A somewhat longer grace period was accorded weekend guests, but not by much. One visitor who was late departing overheard his host telling his dog, in tones of deep satisfaction, "Isn't it lovely, they've all gone." Yet, Margaret Slythe continued, "If they don't come he says very sadly, 'No one comes here now.' " In fairness to him, his days were so full they had to be timed to the minute, with unvarying periods parceled out for correspondence, dictating, phone calls, writing, meetings, lectures, walks, the afternoon nap, the occasional toddle along to the pub for a jug of beer, and his secret vice, girlfriends. I would learn just how much of a pouncer he was; fortunately for me, that aspect of his enthusiasm was fleeting. One had to wonder, given his passion for the stopwatch, how satisfactory he was as a lover. This charming, if mistaken, belief that whatever needed doing in life could be done in ten minutes had its drawbacks, as I would discover when

I wrote his biography. By the time that all came about, I had written two other successful biographies, *Between Me and Life: A Biography of Romaine Brooks,* and *Being Bernard Berenson.* The latter was nominated for a Pulitzer Prize in 1980. I won a Guggenheim Fellowship at the same time, and started thinking I could do no wrong. That was my first mistake.

Like Kenneth Clark, I was an only child. I was born in Bath and grew up on the slopes of the southern hills, in a new semidetached to which my parents moved when I was six years old. The street, Sladebrook Road, was in the sporadic state of being developed that was common following the Great Depression; a few scattered farmhouses built of Bath limestone clung to its rocky sides, with orchards and fields behind them. Down below in the valley, the famous nursery, Blackmore and Langdon, grew spectacular delphiniums in ideal conditions. Sladebrook Road had not been paved, a situation that continued until well after World War II, and my father would drive our motorbike and sidecar down the road, moaning about his springs. I would push my bike up the miniature hills and valleys and, daringly, take a rollercoaster ride back down again. I loved that unpaved road. One could build whole continents on its typography, with streams, rivers and lakes; a spot of oil in the water became, when you stirred it, an iridescent rainbow of colors.

The small-time builder who designed "Westhill" followed the invariable pattern of such semidetached buildings, sometimes called Metroland Suburban, and owing its origins to Charles Voysey. Its roof would be covered with tiles, and there were always bay windows, projecting gables and sometimes half-timbered façades. The front door might be decorated with a panel of stained glass depicting a ship in full sail; sunbursts were also the rage. The semidetached was the equivalent of the American center-hall Colonial. One could predict, without ever entering, the staircase running up directly behind the front door, the formal front room, less formal dining room and sparsely equipped kitchen. There would be three bedrooms and one bathroom upstairs. There was, of course, no central heating, so there were fireplaces in every room. The water pipes were placed considerately outside the walls, so that when water froze in the toilet and the pipes burst, the coagulating drips formed interesting but harmless stalactites on the outside.

Ours was a very scaled-down adaptation of the Voysey original. We did not have anything as grand as half-timbering, or even a stained-glass insert in the front door. We did have a wooden gate with a sunburst pattern and we also had Voysey-designed, heavily paneled interior doors, with handles set at chest height that I could not reach for quite a while. The fireplaces, designed for coal, were miniature, and surrounded by glazed china blocks in a muddy orange, curiously ascending in steps to form a very low mantelpiece. Everywhere, the wood was chocolate brown. The chocolate-brown picture rails would be outlined with a wallpaper border, usually some abstracted design of vine leaves or fruit, very Art Deco, under the rail and up and down the corners. Walls were papered with something the color of porridge, and the yearly papering became an event in which I learned to take part, if only to separate my parents when my mother burst into storms of frustrated tears.

Everything else was brown, buff, beige, coffee or fawn, bedrooms excepted (these were either pink or blue). The matching set of leather sofa and armchairs in the front room was brown. The mock Tudor sideboard was brown. My father's special chair was upholstered in brown. The front-room curtains were light brown, with a silky, feathery leaf pattern. Even the barrel-shaped biscuit tin was brown, and it is no wonder I haven't been able to look at that color since. I left the house with relief and not the slightest inkling that it would haunt me over the years. I dreamt one time that it was being enlarged at the back, with a big pic-

ture window. To my amazement I discovered on my next trip
that this was the case. In my dreams I find myself buying it, and
starting all over again.

It was very small: twelve feet wide by twenty-five feet long.
To my six-year-old eyes it looked enormous. The day we moved
in, my parents put a mattress on the pocket-sized lawn for us to
sit on, and there we had our tea. It was a great day.

The field behind us sloped down to the Blackmore and Langdon valley, giving an uninterrupted and dazzling vista all over
the city of Bath. You could make out the Royal Crescent, the
Circus and Lansdown Crescent on the hills opposite, along with
Victoria Park, Lansdown Road and Beckford's Monument on
the skyline. Our future garden was some seventy-five feet long,
and my father set to work with a will. He put blackberry bushes
along the bottom, planted a plum tree, started a compost heap,
and in time produced amazing amounts of vegetables and fruits:
gooseberries, red and black currants, strawberries, plums, potatoes, onions, carrots, cabbages, brussels sprouts, runner beans
and the sweet peas that Mother brought into the house. If there
is anything better than new potatoes the size of golf balls, dug up
and immediately cooked, or strawberries picked in the morning
sunlight, I don't know what it is.

I spent much of my childhood in the back garden. In my
mind's eye I can see the plum tree, its leaves cracked and drying,
the thick banks of thistles, the mud-caked flowerpots, the rain
barrel, the two stone rabbits on a stump and the calves grazing in
the fields beyond. I see my father, who has had his tea and read
the evening paper, out digging. My mother is checking on the
strings of laundry flapping in the breeze, white butterflies are
fluttering over the cabbages and I am looking for the brown-
and-yellow-striped caterpillars that I will train as my racing
stock. My mother had left Horstmann Gear (it was a point of
pride in those days if a wife did not have to work), and she
became a pretty good cook, seamstress and all-around craftsper-

"Gesturing toward a rose": Olive Doman,
the author's mother

son. She made the curtains and hooked the rugs. She sewed all my clothes and her own. She knitted cardigans, jumpers, hats, gloves and scarves. She embroidered tablecloths and napkins, and on the leather upholstery she put doilies depicting ladies in sunbonnets and crinolines incongruously and daintily watering their gardens. She was a natural gardener, and trained a rambling red rose up the wall beside the front door. I have a photograph of her standing beside it, wearing her best dress and high-heeled shoes, gesturing toward a rose.

There was a brief period when she would draw up a chair and place a tray on it and we would have tea and crumpets before the fireplace in the front room, just the two of us. But once the war came the front room was closed for the duration. Unfortunately we owned a spare bedroom, which was requisitioned for two war workers. These turned out to be Eileen Baker and Florence Prynne, young and pretty Cornish girls who had been in service and were now working on the Horstmann Gear assembly line. I used to watch in amazement as the two of them were transformed by the bedtime ritual into something from which a young husband would recoil in horror. Skin slathered with thick layers of night cream, their hair done up in curlers, topped by pink and blue nets, their feet in furry socks, they would retire hopefully to bed. I say hopefully, because I never could discern any difference in the morning.

So the house was already crowded when my paternal grandmother died and my grandfather came to join us. He took my bedroom; I moved in with Eileen and Florrie. All that crowding should have made life intolerable but, curiously, did not. The attitude was that we were all in the same boat. My mother enjoyed their company, and the girls were extremely good about helping her. Sunday lunch was the great moment of the week. The three of them would disappear into the kitchen and shut the door. After much chattering and giggling, there would be sumptuous smells of roast beef and Yorkshire pudding, with apple pie to follow, and they would emerge red-faced and triumphant.

Before they got the motorbike and sidecar, my parents' idea of a scintillating Sunday afternoon was to go for a walk. The city of Bath lies in a winding river valley, with hills on all sides; our usual path brought us down from the hills to the south and along the Upper Bristol Road, where my parents had a flat when they first got married. There was always a stop at the children's playground in the lower end of Victoria Park, and then I would have to endure a lengthy exploration of the Botanic Gardens in the upper corner, with much anxious consulting of tiny labels, while I waited impatiently for the trip to arrive at the fishpond farther down the park. Just across the road from there, one had a clear view of the Royal Crescent in all its classical Georgian grandeur, elegant, restrained and magnificent, framed by sweeping fields, lawns and handsome trees. If you walked down Royal Avenue through the park, you eventually came to the tennis courts, where I played many a late afternoon, panting and squinting with the sun in my eyes. My maternal grandmother, Gran Bird, had a basement flat around the corner in Charlotte Street, just down from the Christian Science Church, wrongly thought to be modeled after the Temple of Vesta at Tivoli.

Then you walked up Gay Street to the Circus, the masterpiece John Wood the Elder had built as part of his romantic vision to make Bath an embodiment of ancient Rome. You skipped along Bennett Street, right past the Assembly Rooms. To a child's eye, these rooms look closed and secretive and it was only later that I realized what glorious interiors they were hiding from view. I was headed for my special place, a flight of steps descending past small antiques shops on the left and the old Evans and Owen department store (est. 1846) on the right, to the top of Milsom Street. There from its wide, terraced stone pavement one had an unhindered view over the lower city with a glimpse of the green slopes of Beechen Cliff rising behind it.

Thanks to laws passed after World War II, Bath has retained its bucolic setting and, along with it, the eighteenth-century concept of the pastoral that ennobles its poetry and is implicit in paintings by Gainsborough and Reynolds. The two John Woods, father and son, Thomas Baldwin, James Wilson and George Philip Manners were among the architects who transformed a scruffy little medieval city with neglected Roman ruins into a unified concept of eighteenth-century town planning. It was a city built for pleasure—gambling, dancing and womanizing—but not pleasure alone, because, to the eighteenth-century mind, beauty had an instructive function if not a moral one.

The Circus, Bath. A watercolor by A. Woodroffe, c. 1820

Milsom Street, Bath, in Jane Austen's Day,
by A. Woodroffe, c. 1820

Such circles, squares, avenues and terraces, recalling the splendors of Rome and expressed in the architectural language of Palladio, would please the eye and elevate the mind. All of this was set against a background of green, because nature also had an ennobling effect. In a sense the city itself was envisioned as surrounded by a park (touched up a bit by Capability Brown, perhaps). Aristocratic visitors, and they all came, would expect no less; commoners might also be edified and instructed. So the enveloping slopes of woods and valleys, with their quaint Roman fosse ways, ancient coppices and wansdykes, their groves and bosky dells, were as much a part of the concept as were the buildings themselves.

And what buildings they were. The hills around Bath were being mined for a particular honey-colored limestone, not particularly durable and easily stained, but ravishingly lovely in the soft West Country light. The long flights of houses, magnificent crescents like Lansdown and Camden, Norfolk and Cavendish, were the set pieces, but more modest terraces, descending in graceful arcs down the hillsides, had their own charm, as did Beaufort Square, Quiet Street and Marlborough buildings. These might vary in scale and importance, but all had the merit of treating their façades with a single unifying scheme. So, in the case of the Circus and the Royal Crescent, one finds a continuous colonnade of columns, with appropriate entablatures and friezes, broken at the right intervals with precisely placed windows and doors. Behind the façades the owners were at liberty to do whatever they liked, and the backs of some of these buildings have the higgledy-piggledy look one would expect from exasperated tenants giving vent to their frustrations. But in front, all was restraint, balance and elegant understatement. The pavements were wide, the vistas amazing, the streets cobbled, and sheep grazed on the grass in front of the Royal Crescent. It was an unsullied vision of Arcadia.

Et in Arcadia ego . . . : the knowledge came slowly. Before

"An unsullied vision of Arcadia": the Royal and
Lansdown Crescents by A. Watts

World War II, Bath's magnificence was less evident. Everyone
burned coal, and acids in the smoke ate away at the beautiful
detailing and streaked the old stones with smears and drips, as if
some giant hand had produced unreadable graffiti. After its century of glamour as the haunt of royalty and the aristocracy, of
Jane Austen, Charles Dickens, General Wolfe, Richard Brinsley
Sheridan, Alexander Pope and William Pitt, Bath slid with infinite slowness into a kind of decayed respectability. Aging gentle-
women, retired civil servants, admirals and others on limited
incomes came to spend their declining years in Bath. They lived
in flats hurriedly carved out of houses built for single families,
with lavatories squeezed onto half-landings in the French fashion, uncomfortable kitchens with hot plates and no plumbing,
and doors cut out of once-solid walls. Before the Royal Crescent
Hotel made its transformations, I visited the sorry inn that
inhabited the same space and was shocked to find huge rooms
cut up into cubicles, and mean-looking imitations of Danish

modern in the bedrooms. But that was Bath until recently: a city of lost genius. Taking a stroll in Victoria Park, one used to see a very old lady whose silhouette had, in her youth, been deformed into the once-fashionable swanlike shape in which she was doomed to live out her declining years; her fate seemed symbolic. And yet this lovely, crumbling, battered and deserted town, defaced with grime, insulted by ignorance and willful vandalism, was still, in all essential respects, as beautiful as it had been in the days of Gainsborough and Beau Nash. Until the 1950s, it was among the two or three complete period cities in the world.

So we took our Saturday morning coffee at The Canary in Queen Street or at the Pump Room in the Abbey Churchyard. Water was still being dispensed there, as it had since the eighteenth century, coming from hot springs that had gushed up half a million gallons a day since time immemorial. It was said to be good for rheumatism, sterility and heaven knows what else. One swallow and we shunned it for the rest of our lives; it tasted like warm flatirons. The Pump Room was the scene of weekly dances, and when I got older I would go there, lining up with giggling friends on one side of the room while the boys, glowering and uncertain, lined up on the other. We went to Mallory's for silver and to Pugsley's for our open-cut suede sandals by Clark's. We had fish and chips at Evans' Restaurant, went to the Old Red House (est. 1798) for tea and cakes, and to Jolly's in Milsom Street for everything else, following a sedate round that had probably changed little for two hundred years. We went to the Theatre Royal for the annual pantomime or to hear Donald Wolfit, playing Othello, Lear or Macbeth, thunder from its tradition-haunted stage. We listened to the brass bands in the Parade Gardens on Sunday afternoons, or, rather, my parents sat in deck chairs while I explored the hidden pet cemetery in the park and copied out the epitaphs on tiny tombstones for Fido, Flossie and Frabjous. We bought Japanese paper parasols and

Evening in Paris perfume at Woolworth's. We chose our Saturday morning fruit from the stalls outside St. James's Church at the intersection of Stall and Southgate streets, never failing to admire its pretty cupola. That church was hit during the bombing of Bath, and what the Germans did not destroy, the city of Bath finished off, and much else. The church and the street beside it disappeared, swallowed up in 1957 by a huge Marks & Spencer. Architecture derived from the Bauhaus, brutal blocks of stone (the Beaufort Hotel and car park), replaced the eighteenth-century buildings in Northgate Street. Seventeenth- and eighteenth-century houses were demolished in Holloway to make way for blocks of flats that one architect said looked like chicken coops, and the desecrations were widely repeated. But the defacement that is most obvious to the casual visitor is the demolition of most of Stall Street, replacing the period buildings with a tawdry mall, along with a squat and nasty bus station behind it. Only a national outcry prevented the wrecking gangs from leveling the rest of the city and constructing a superhighway through it.

By the time Bath was doing its best to destroy itself, Bath as a concept had become as natural to me as breathing. I loved everything about it, even those traces of the medieval city that survive in fragments of a wall and in the meandering courts, passages and lanes, quirky and unexpected, that beckon one onward, promising new discoveries and hidden treasures. I marveled at the terraced pavements on Lansdown Road and the elegant changes of level that were handled with such deftness by the old architects. The design of railings, ironwork, brackets and metopes gave me my first serendipitous lessons in coherence of style that have informed my taste ever since. As for those Utopian visions of stability, balance, and harmony, the great buildings with their complex symmetry, refined proportions and decorative invention, these were inexhaustible pleasures. As I walked along the streets it seemed to me that each set of windows and doors was another interval marking my passage into young womanhood. Their repetitious images sank into the mental layer between dreams and awakening, when one is always dancing and turning; the room is swaying, the crystal chandeliers wink and beckon, and there are trees outside the window. In *Moments of Vision,* Kenneth Clark wrote, "So Ruskin discovered his responsiveness to sparkle and filigree—to fireflies and twig tracery; and Coleridge surrendered himself to the pale transparency of the moon."

Chapter Two

Through the Keyhole with K.C.

I had not realized how difficult writing a biography of Kenneth Clark would be until, in the autumn of 1978, I began work. By then he had taken an avuncular interest in my first biography, about the artist Romaine Brooks, and was actively helping my study of Berenson, at whose feet he had sat in the 1920s, during several months spent at the latter's Italian villa. In terms of the art market, he knew exactly where the bodies were buried. Once K had read the resulting manuscript, he readily provided a flattering blurb. Further, he said I could write about him, something I had previously suggested and that he had waved aside with the disingenuous comment that no one would want to read the book. There was no shortage of publishing interest. I had a bright young editor, Jennifer Josephy, at Holt, Rinehart & Winston in New York, and for the first, and last, time, two publishers in London. They were Weidenfeld & Nicolson, which was publishing *Being Bernard Berenson,* and John Murray, Kenneth Clark's own publisher. Both were providing a comfortable advance, and it all seemed aboveboard until I ran into David Carritt. He was a brilliant and much-feared London art dealer in the world of Old Masters whom I had already interviewed for whatever he knew about Berenson, which was quite a bit. He

Kenneth Clark, 1979

said it was "all over London" that Kenneth Clark was putting up money for the book. I indignantly denied this. That K could be slipping money under the table seemed impossible, unthinkable really, and I dismissed his comment. Later—all too late—I discovered how right he was.

There had been a John Murray ever since that august house on Albemarle Street, founded in 1768, had published Byron. "Jock" Murray, as he was known, was a Murray on his mother's side, born John Arnaud Robin Grey, who changed his name to Murray when he took over the family business. His friendship with Kenneth Clark began when he praised and published an early work, *The Gothic Revival;* K gave him all the others.

23

By the time I met him, Jock Murray had been running his publishing house for decades and was a familiar figure, with his natty bow ties, his free-floating eyebrows, which seemed to have a life of their own, and a quizzical, always benevolent expression. I first caught sight of his agile figure halfway up the steep stairs of the publishing house that seemed, in retrospect, a metaphor. His job, as I already knew, was to protect K from me, and he was ever alert to signs of insubordination. Early in my manuscript, describing Kenneth Clark as a young man in the 1930s when sleek hair was all the rage, I used the term "slicked back." That would not do at all, and I knew Jock Murray was going to be trouble. Still, I liked him; like K himself, he had impeccable old-fashioned manners along with a distrust of newfangled gadgets of any description; he barely tolerated typewriters. When obliged to make use of a transatlantic telephone, he would ask, "Have you got Mrs. Secrest there?" as if he fully expected the answer to be no. He was totally loyal, yet, was he all that loyal? Some time later, when the whole project began to go wrong, I was invited to the Murrays' for dinner to meet John Hale, the art historian who had praised my book on Berenson, and his wife Sheila. By then Jock had a copy of K's emendations, written in a shaky hand. After lecturing me for being so intransigent, Jock commented that the manuscript, with its indignant criticisms, would one day be worth a lot of money. There was no doubt that he enjoyed the prospect hugely.

Murray was naturally conversant with the byzantine workings of the Clark family and its circle of acquaintances, and knew the whole story from firsthand experience. From the beginning he was determined to warn me about people who disliked Kenneth Clark, thinking him arrogant and aloof, and would paint every flaw in Technicolor.

The Clarks had three children: Alan, the oldest, and the twins, Colette and Colin. Jock Murray did not think the twins would present a problem, but was very concerned about Alan. He insisted that I get a letter from K instructing his heirs not to

Kenneth Clark, at right, with Graham Sutherland,
John Piper, and Henry Moore

meddle with my text. Otherwise he thought Alan, whom he called an "angular" character (others said he was "to the right of Attila the Hun"), would cause trouble. There were other issues, i.e., getting K to say something new about subjects that he had not already exhausted in *Another Part of the Wood* and its lame sequel, *The Other Half.*

Then there was the matter of the right emphasis. It was true that *Civilisation* (some thought it should have been called *The History of Art in Western Europe*) had reached an international audience with its sweeping and provocative parallels between historical events and the development of European culture. The book had sold over a million copies and the film series had been viewed by a vast public.

But there was a danger of slighting his other achievements: as a young and energetic bureaucrat, shaking up hidebound institutions like the National Gallery; his role as patron of young artists like Victor Pasmore, Graham Sutherland and Henry Moore; his influence on Buckingham Palace taste; his beautifully written books; and his galvanizing effect on audiences as a lecturer. There was a reason why he had seemed so familiar when I met him in David Finley's drawing room in Georgetown. I had seen him lecture myself and completely forgotten about it.

It all happened as I entered sixth form at the City of Bath Girls' School. Just after World War II, we seniors were invited to attend a national conference in London being given by the Council for Education in World Citizenship, at which a number of famous men would give talks about the future of Germany, the defects of the Treaty of Versailles, the economic impact of trade unionism, and other esoterica over which I had not bothered my fairly empty head.

I wish I could say that the experience of hearing J. B. Priestley, Harold Nicolson, Harold Laski, et al., changed my worldview or, at least, impressed on me the idea that I ought to have a worldview. I do not remember a thing about their speeches. What I do remember is a speaker whose name I did not catch.

Kenneth Clark with Queen Elizabeth, listening to a concert at the National Gallery, London, in wartime

Everything about him fascinated me: the neat head with its even features, the smooth and shining hair, the energy of movement, the rapidity of emphasis, and a certain look that would sometimes cross his face; it seemed infinitely endearing. I was seduced, no question about it. Amazing concepts flashed through my mind. Art, poetry and music wove their way in and out of his sentences, provocative ideas and hidden paradoxes, like the seriousness of pleasure, the irrational nature of creativity, the melancholy underlying Mozart's music and, particularly, a philosophical and mystical approach to art that was in harmony with my own romantic view. He seemed to be standing in his own spotlight. It was a phenomenon I only saw once more, when, just after he had been elected to the presidency, John F. Kennedy arrived at National Airport in Washington. He came out of the plane door and stood at the top of the boarding steps. He smiled, and the crowd roared. This speaker had much the same effect on me. That was the day I resolved to dedicate myself to art. And I had completely forgotten his name. Now that I had made the connection, how could I give full weight to his passionate intensity, this glimpse of the transcendental nature of art that he had shown me and so many others? That seemed the most daunting challenge of all.

In the years following our meeting in 1969, I had visited K on my trips to Britain and knew that he had given Saltwood Castle to his son Alan, his wife, Jane, and their two sons, and built a house on the castle grounds. This was an ingeniously designed one-floor villa, vaguely modernist in feeling and cautious in execution. It was saved from banality by the expansiveness of its rooms, plenty of windows and the owner's decor: William Morris reproduction wallpaper in softening arabesques and contrapuntal curves. The Clark art collection, surprisingly, looked better than it had in the castle, if only because of the light and less architectural distraction. There was a small, perfect self-portrait by Samuel Palmer, a Jack Yeats painting of a rose floating in a washbasin (thoughtfully placed in a bathroom), a

Vanessa Bell self-portrait, and a small, powerful Rodin bronze. There were many more important items to admire: a Victor Pasmore odalisque in homage to Ingres, a Degas of a woman bathing, and K's most loved and treasured painting, *Seascape: Folkestone*, by Turner. Clark devoted much time and thought to this unjustly neglected painter, as he believed. "I feel that many of Turner's most moving works were done in . . . [a] condition of dreamlike ecstasy. . . ." When Kenneth Clark's collection was sold a year after his death (June–July 1984), his heirs kept the Degas and Palmer, but Sotheby's sold enough other works to keep sales going for three days. The final item sold was the Turner, which Alan Clark frequently called his father's favorite. He had no feeling about it whatsoever, he told the press, but privately expressed satisfaction about selling the one thing his father loved best. At the eleventh hour his brother Colin stepped forward with an action to stop the sale. He claimed the Turner had been left to him in his father's will. (He was right.) Obviously something had to be done immediately, and a settlement was reached to his financial satisfaction, to judge from Colin's broad smile when the painting went on the block. It sold for a record price, £7.3 million, or $10 million.

After *Civilisation*, K was in fine form, but each time we met, there seemed to be an imperceptible downward shift of mood. When I visited them in the summer of 1974 I learned that Jane had had a stroke and was partly paralyzed. She insisted on dressing for the occasion, and was wheeled into the garden wearing a fifties-looking, yellow-and-white-checked cotton dress and floppy, broad-brimmed, yellow-and-white-checked cotton hat. I was so unnerved by this apparition, which would have looked *jeune fille* even on an ingénue, that I could not think of a word to say. While I struggled, K, breathing hard, gamely tried to push Jane and her wheelchair over the bumpy grass.

Two years after that, in the spring of 1976, I returned to the Garden House, as it was called, to talk about Berenson. Jane was now confined to her bedroom. After trying, and failing, to walk again, she seemed to have gone mad. She was cursing God; K was horrified. That blustery spring afternoon he went for his usual walk in the castle grounds and I tagged along behind him. The wind ripped through our clothes, the peacocks screamed, and his mouth was drawn into a bitter line. He was at his wits' end. He dared not leave Jane alone for a moment. The odd thing was, he said, that his funniest passages in *Another Part of the Wood* had been written at moments of deepest despair.

Just after K finished his second volume of autobiography, Jane died. There was a year of bachelorhood and then, to everyone's surprise, in the autumn of 1977 he married again. She was Nolwen de Janzé Rice, a widow he had known for some years, daughter of a French count and owner of an ancient Norman estate. Writing to tell me, K made the quaint comment that Nolwen's lineage was so distinguished she might be considered

Kenneth Clark and the second Lady Clark,
the former Nolwen de Janzé Rice

to be "marrying beneath her." Since Nolwen had also watched her partner die by inches, that they should be brought together in their mutual misery and bereavement seemed understandable. Then, on the eve of their marriage, K told his bride-to-be that he, too, was ill and needed an immediate operation on his prostate. It was not a propitious beginning, complicated by the fact that another lady friend of very long standing, Janet Stone, herself a widow, had assumed a prominent role during his year alone. She appeared outside his hospital room prepared to take over the direction of his care. The discussion that followed was pretty animated. The new wife won.

I arrived to begin work on the project in the autumn of 1978, and was met at the Sandling train station by Kenneth Clark. My diaries note that he praised my book on Berenson so extravagantly—"you got it exactly right"—that I found myself in tears. I spoke briefly to Nolwen, who was recovering from a bout of brucellosis that she, as a dairy farmer, had contracted from her cows. We began work at once. He said he was aware that his autobiography, particularly the second volume, was incomplete because "there were things I couldn't say," but he did not see any area of his life that was off limits, as it were. In the months that followed, I asked him for a letter confirming my editorial independence and we went back and forth on this. He did not see a problem but would quite like to check the manuscript for errors of fact. His explanation was given with good humor and seemed reasonable, but the resulting letter of permission, written for his literary executor—Alan Clark, as it turned out—was disappointing. The wording given was that the author naturally wanted to be free in the matter of opinion and he "hoped" his literary executor would respect his wishes. When I showed the letter to Jock Murray, he was not happy about it either, but agreed it was probably the best we could do.

Jane Clark in later years: "the great untold story"

It was immediately clear to me that the theme that should have dominated *The Other Half,* but didn't, was Jane's drinking. (I found it revealing that Kenneth Clark should have chosen that particular title, given its common reference to a wife.) In fact the great untold story was the role she had played in his life, the gradual onset of her addiction, its consequences for himself and the children, its destructive impact, and its notoriety, after all those times when she had been publicly and flauntingly drunk. Had he not seen this dilemma as a repetition of the one he had been obliged to endure with his own much-loved father, who was another public drunk? To make matters worse, his emotionally distant mother had forced him, as a small boy, to find his father and get him into taxis and up to bed. He had said as much in his first volume, but had not revealed the extent to which it had upset and humiliated him. And of course he could say nothing about Jane in *The Other Half* because she was still alive and wanting to read every word. His refusal to tackle the subject—he told Colette he had once attempted it, but Jane had "bitten his head off"—told me something about his evasiveness and horror of scenes. His children, on the other hand, seemed almost embarrassingly ready to describe Mama's derelictions in the kind of Technicolor that Jock Murray had warned me against: her rages, her emotional needs, her childishness and her unnerving ability to switch moods on and off. They thought she must be schizoid.

His life with Jane seemed to be one of the stories K had wanted me to write. I could never be sure, and he never hinted a word to that effect. But he answered every question with enough zest to make me think he had been waiting for it. He had no guilty feelings whatsoever; "I was absolutely sweet to her and looked after her like an angel," he told me, and this was true.

At the same time, something odd seemed to be happening. His children made it clear that a sober Jane was loud and argumentative. Booze acted as a tranquilizer, and she became calmer and calmer until, as I witnessed, she went fuzzily off to bed. That was the moment when K, who had been shouted down, took over. So letting her drink had its large compensations: he came into his own. I also began to get hints from others of the extent to which he aided and abetted this transformation. Even when her illness was far advanced, Mr. Linley, K's factotum, would see his employer trotting down the hall at ten in the morning with her first "tranquilizer" of the day in his hand. This worried me. As I understood it, alcoholism was believed to have its origins in a genetic predisposition, but deep-seated emotional problems also played a role. I knew that this was not the view of K himself or any of his contemporaries, my father's generation. To them excessive drinking was a failure of the will, a moral flaw. Seen in that light, what Kenneth Clark endured was heroic. The idea of mine that Jane had a problem that she was powerless to solve alone, but that K also had a problem in his willingness to aid and abet it, was not going to go down well. Least of all with him.

Then there were all those ladies, not just Janet Stone, in whom he confided for years, but others equally charmed, as I had been, by the vigor, sparkle and erudition of his personality, along with that certain look. Nolwen was forthright about the degrees of feeling that had led her from a grateful kind of friendship into love. She talked about his operation, which had left him impotent; he had only been able to prove his love for her twice, she said, but that did not matter because what they shared was so much more important. "I'll take him on any terms." She was much taken aback by the reaction of K's women friends to his marriage. She would answer the phone and someone on the other end would hang up. "They didn't take it like you, Meryle; they weren't as generous and happy for him." I was a bit bemused by the compliment, not considering myself in that company. K, who happened to be in the room at that point, listened tolerantly, saying little except that she had exaggerated their numbers. He referred to himself, chuckling, as "an old rake." He seemed rather to enjoy being fought over. I wondered who they could all be. When I unearthed the artist Mary Kessell, with whom K had had a long affair—it was the old-fashioned arrangement, complete with apartment and living allowance— he was not happy about it and he never did talk about Janet Stone. Or anyone else.

But the aspect of the story that really bothered me, not to mention my two editors, Jock Murray and John Curtis of Weidenfeld, was the echo effect. That is to say, all the stories K was telling me that he had already published in his memoirs, usually word for word. His anecdotes had settled into well-worn grooves, as so often happens with people who have been inter-viewed too much. The façade had become the man. More than once, very courteously, he had mentioned that he knew perfectly well I was trying to probe beneath the surface, but there was nothing there. I had arrived at the stage in our relationship when a dismissive wave of the hand told me there was plenty there, just nothing he wanted to talk about. By then I'd been inter-viewing people for a few years and knew that with a really tough customer my only hope was to disarm him or her. But I was at a disadvantage: I was living on one continent and he on another. So my visits were bound to be heralded well in advance, by which time he would have built up whatever defenses I had managed to break down during the previous encounters, and I would have to start all over again. I got more and more evasive and cunning, and a dawning look would come into his eye and he would be evasive and cunning right back. I've never played chess, but I imagine it was like that. You make a move and either catch your opponent off guard or be wiped off the board. And I was dealing with a master.

In fairness to him, he really had forgotten a great deal. It helped to talk with the dwindling band of contemporaries, a few of whom had known him since their Winchester and Oxford days, and who could recall moments he had forgotten. I could not have known he was suffering from the early symptoms of Parkinson's disease, which affects the mind in unsettling ways. Such vignettes from others would often evoke a surprising response, but they were few. He was not only wary of self-revelation but deviously clever about getting his own way. I was with him once when Nolwen went to visit her dressmaker, leav-ing K and me waiting in the car. K decided she was taking too long. So he got out and, waving a tantalizing newspaper, had every watchdog in that canine-populated neighborhood barking its head off. She emerged, apologetic, a few moments later. There was a curious tug-of-war going on between them that cen-tered around the fact that she had a farm to run in Normandy

Alan Clark, his wife Jane, and Kenneth Clark,
outside the Garden House

and he liked to stay in Kent. When at the Garden House, she, bored, tried to get things done; according to her, Mr. Linley resisted her ideas or any change at all. When in Parfondeval, K, who was equally bored, began looking for ways to assert control, sometimes quite unconsciously. I was a guest there one weekend with Sir Colin and Lady Anderson, whose roles were, I assumed, to shake loose a few more of K's memories. The five of us were about to have dinner when Nolwen, who, as the host, sat at the head of the table, was called to the kitchen for a last-minute conference. K immediately took over. "I'll sit here," he said, indicating Nolwen's seat. "Meryle, you sit on my left. Morna [Lady Anderson], you sit on my right. Colin, you sit next to Meryle." He paused. "But I thought there were five of us." Just then, Lady Clark entered the room.

As for Alan Clark, Margaret Slythe, another old friend of his father's, warned me not to alienate him. He was bound to feel jealous, she said, because, "He will think he is the one who should write his father's biography, not you." And I knew that Alan Clark was a fine stylist, having written several highly regarded books on military history. There was *The Fall of Crete, The Donkeys* (about the disastrous British Expeditionary Force in World War I, which gave rise to the Joan Littlewood satire *Oh What a Lovely War!*) and *Barbarossa,* about the Nazi-Soviet conflict of 1941–45. I had also heard of his admiration for Hitler, as well as rumors that the hall of Saltwood Castle was hung with SS banners and one of his dogs was named after Eva Braun. What his father, who had thrown every effort into fighting Nazi Germany, must have thought of all this I couldn't bear to think. "Alan wants to be known as the gauleiter of Kent," another friend remarked. Was it all just nose-thumbing? On the surface, he was living a very correct life indeed with his wife and sons, his fifty-room castle in Kent, an apartment in Albany, a Scottish estate, a chalet in Zermatt, no shortage of money, and in the early stages of a prominent political career.

I was very much on my guard, and was taken aback to find an unprepossessing person in his early fifties who almost slid into the room. In youth he had been dashingly handsome, but now his features had blunted and thickened. There was *un pli amer,* a bitter pleat, around the mouth and there were frown lines between the eyes, although he seemed cordial enough, in an off-hand and ever so slightly condescending way. He looked like a more squarely built, athletic version of his father, which indeed he was, being an expert swimmer and skier and lover of vintage Jaguar sports cars (the SS-100, the C-Type and the XK), in goggles and with a cap jammed down over his eyes.

He began by saying he did not care what I wrote; I could not hurt his feelings. He then, surprisingly, launched into a detailed description of a lonely and loveless childhood. He was sent away to boarding school and nobody cared; "They *expected* you to be unhappy," he said emphatically. His mother hated him and as good as told him so. He said, "I flinched when she touched me."

He sat in a far corner of the room, arms folded, hugging himself. Eton was, he wrote later, "an early introduction to human cruelty, treachery and extreme physical hardship." As for Christ Church, Oxford, that was "a waste of time and petrol." Almost the only good experience of his youth was when he worked his way across the United States, picking up odd jobs and waiting on tables. He was completely happy for the first time.

His feelings about his father were conflicted. He could not remember his father ever rising to his defense. And he never asked for help: "I might have tried, but there was a tacit understanding that 'one didn't.' " His father was a wonderful friend and "just occasionally you got a kind of intimacy . . ." His most poignant fear was that his father would die without his being able to show him how much he loved him. At the same time there was anger and resentment. "Do you want to know where my father's love letters are? They're in there," he said roughly, gesturing toward a cabinet. (He was right.) A few months after that he wanted me to read a review by Christopher Booker of *The Other Half.* I followed him into his study; it was the first time I had visited Saltwood Castle since the change of administration. The contrast could not have been more striking; it seemed to have been taken over by clever and capricious children. I did not see any SS banners hanging in the hall, but there were muddles everywhere. In particular, Clark's study was in chaos, with drawers open and overflowing and papers strewn across the carpet. When he found the review, he pointed out one criticism in particular: "As the picture of a man who to the end of his life has never dared face up to 'the other half' of himself, this is a spine-chilling book." This was evidently what Alan Clark really thought of his father. As for his mother, and the three years it took her to die, he told me what he used to say: "Why doesn't she get on with it?"

He just knew that his mother had committed suicide. She took an overdose of sleeping pills. Well, because she wrote farewell letters to everyone, he said. Her doctor would confirm this. He gave me an address for Dr. Raymond Rowntree that turned out to be twelve years out of date. I got in touch with the good doctor, but, as I expected, he would say nothing—for legal reasons, he explained. If Alan Clark would write and give him permission, he could tell me more. Alan Clark's reply to my query did not provide that permission. All he would say was that Dr. Rowntree "had put it to me in the form of an assumption which no one could question." He seemed to revel in dramatic accusations, whether about suicide or murder. Some years later, in 1993, Alan Clark published his journals, in which he claimed that Nolwen had killed his father: "The fool of a doctor can't see, or won't accept that Nolwen is poisoning him," he wrote in 1983, after his father was diagnosed with diverticulitis. Another entry, for July 13, 1990, noted that this was his father's birthday. "He would be eighty-seven today, if Nolwen hadn't poisoned him." Not a single reviewer seems to have noticed, let alone challenged this outrageous assertion. Well, you can't libel the dead, and by the time of publication, both K and Nolwen had died. Everyone knew that Alan Clark was a shameless show-off, full of bluster and hot air, and so no one took him seriously; was that it? Such a comment, had it been published during K's lifetime, would have horrified him. In many ways they were opposed tempera-ments, a distinction Alan seemed anxious to further. And yet, were there certain parallels between father and son? Could one say of them, as Cyril Connolly did of himself after leaving Eton, that "the greater part of the ruling class remains adolescent, school-minded, self-conscious, cowardly [and] sentimental"? Alan Clark conceded the adolescent part when he told journal-ists he was "sixty-five going on sixteen." To which his wife added, "Sixty-five going on twelve."

The problem about writing the life of someone who is still alive is the pall it casts over the narrative, since you are well aware that every word will be analyzed and searched for a hidden meaning. This puts paid to the fine, flowing spontaneity with which you hope to write, and is necessary if the reader is to gain confidence in you as an observer. What was evidently appropriate here was the guarded statement, an ability to make a criticism so obliquely that nobody noticed (except the reader). I admire subtlety in writing, but find it hard to be sufficiently devious. The more I wrote, the more my narrative confidence was shriveling, and the whole undertaking began to creak and groan. Since there were ever so many ways to offend K in particular, and since—by now I had some idea of the complicated crosscurrents of feeling—I also had to worry about his family, maybe I should abandon the effort. But that meant paying back publishers' advances, most of which I had spent on the business of going back and forth across the Atlantic. On the other hand, since I could not possibly please everyone, perhaps I should just say what I thought? This was not working either. At this juncture Nolwen let it be known that I was not to make references to any other ladies in his life except, maybe, Jane. Even my subject, with his gift for appeasement, agreed this was an impossible request. Meanwhile, he was responding to my typewritten lists of questions with his usual half-answers and non-answers. He kept asking me to come back.

Going to see K was not much fun either, because his mood, which had been buoyed up by his marriage, was once more falling into a state of melancholy and regret; "thoughts so painful that I cannot face them," he once wrote. The next time I visited, instead of K to meet me at the station it was Nolwen, which was the first shock. He was sitting in the living room, his mouth half open, looking flustered and vague. He had had a *coup de vieux,* he said. I remember exactly when he said it. He was leaning on a cane one gray and sullen autumn day, and we were watching the gulls wheeling over the front in Hythe. His comment filled me with sadness. It was true he was getting absent-minded. Nolwen told me privately that his doctor thought he should no longer drive. This upset him. "Why can't I . . . ?" She was trying to cut back on his drinking, which it is fair to say needed some attention. After a stiff Scotch or two, followed by wine at lunch and dinner, he had forgotten his own name. Nolwen was encouraging him to have a hip operation. This called for stubborn daily demonstrations that he was perfectly capable of rising from low chairs, or even from the floor. Whenever I saw him vainly flailing about and struggling, I offered a surreptitious hand. When Nolwen wasn't watching, of course.

In those final months of Kenneth Clark's life the observer I most trusted was Len Linley, once Margot Fonteyn's chauffeur, who joined the castle staff in 1969 and became Lord Clark's butler and amanuensis. He said of himself, "I came for six months and stayed for fourteen years." By the summer of 1983, Mr. Linley saw Nolwen gradually taking over the management and running of Kenneth Clark's life. She made the plans, chose the menus, paid the bills, sold property and even answered his mail. He was in bed, shakily shuffling between bathroom and kitchen in a dressing gown and slippers, supported on two sticks. She had abrogated his role, but this was also Lord Clark's fault, Linley thought, because of his inability, or refusal, to assert himself. She had planned that they would spend the summer in Parfondeval to be there for a wedding, one frequently postponed because, Mr. Linley thought, Lord Clark kept getting ill to avoid having to go. There was the moment when, Mr. Linley recalled, Lord Clark put his arms around him, a very uncharacteristic gesture indeed, and begged him to prevent this from happening. This, then, was my hero's fatal flaw: the pain, insecurity and doubt that underlay the air of outward self-assurance.

Mr. Linley had cooked for Lord Clark for years and disapproved of the dishes Lady Clark was concocting at night, such as mussels and pigs' trotters, which may have accounted for Alan Clark's claims of sinister intent. She, too, took to spending her

Len Linley

days in a nightdress and gown, eating meals in the kitchen and draping wet laundry about the house, all of which was deeply shocking to Mr. Linley. But the main problem, he thought, was that "she made him feel like a child." In September 1983, some months after Kenneth Clark's death, he put it this way: "Lady Clark thought she understood him, but she didn't. If I'd been able to care for him, he'd still be alive and I don't care who knows it." He knew what Nolwen did not perceive, or chose to ignore: the crucial necessity of letting her husband feel in charge.

Given the right opportunity, Kenneth Clark could recover his old confidence with breathtaking alacrity. In the spring of 1983, Nolwen was obliged to go to France one weekend alone. (She was at pains not to leave K on the perfectly correct assumption that, during his most vulnerable hour, somewhere between five and seven, he would be bound to summon a girlfriend to stave off his loneliness.) K was left in Mr. Linley's charge. When she left on Friday, K was in bed. The next morning Mr. Linley was in the kitchen and heard a noise. He turned and got the shock of his life. Lord Clark was in the doorway, dressed and standing. That was in March, two months before he died.

What I had going for the book, or so I thought, were K's letters. By then I had a handsome collection, not only of his to me—usually written during his many train trips from London to Saltwood and back again—but those to Jane, his parents, Nolwen, and various friends and some prominent girlfriends, including Margaret Slythe and Janet Stone. This last was a photographer and the wife of Reynolds Stone, a much-celebrated wood engraver and calligrapher whose distinctive works influenced decades of bookplates, labels, postage stamps and even five- and ten-pound notes in the days before decimal currency. He, his wife and four children lived in a nineteenth-century rectory in a remote corner of Dorset beside unspoilt valleys and meandering streams from which he extracted his mysterious, emotionally charged miniatures: he always worked on a delicate scale. Janet Stone remained a part of K's life for decades. She was the recipient of several hundred letters and notes. "I was his sink," as she oddly put it. Like Jane Clark, Janet was fearless, a talent K naturally admired. She dashed through life at madcap speed though not always tidily, since she made careless assumptions about things like addresses and telephone numbers. She did, however, reconcile husband to lover and vice versa so successfully that when Jock Murray published a book of Reynolds Stone's engravings, Kenneth Clark wrote an appreciation. It was all very civilized and incestuous.

I eventually came to understand that the degree to which my subject's friends would cooperate, or not, depended in large part on motivations to which I was seldom privy. In Janet Stone's case, her eagerness to let me depart with a thirty-year collection of letters made her own motives clear enough. I knew from others that she considered herself the Great Love of Kenneth Clark's life, and with reason. To have a complete dark horse in the Clark stakes streak across the finish line—my role was practically ordained.

It had been pointed out to me that I was no stylist. (Well, I knew that already.) I therefore could not hope to match or even approach my mentor's flawless prose. I decided, however, that I could write bridging paragraphs and count upon direct quotes from Kenneth Clark's letters to carry the narrative. I certainly had enough of them. It turned out to be a very long manuscript that I, in a lapse of judgment, sent off to K in the summer of 1982.

Jane's addiction evidently needed to be written about in just the right way. It was back to diplomacy, subtlety and nuance, with which one might be able to describe K's ordeal during those years when Jane had strokes and delusions and thought that she was going to marry somebody else and that her skin came off on one's hand. It would not in any way detract from the main focus of the narrative, which would detail his accomplishments. But the fact was that if I were to quote from his letters, these were all about the agony he wanted to keep private.

There were further factors at work. I remember Colette asking whether I was going to tell the truth, and if I was not, why write the book? Her look was challenging, and it made the proper impression. I was determined not to censor or be censored. But I had not reckoned on the effect on my subject of allowing himself to be seen publicly complaining about someone he had long supported and loved. It would look like a betrayal. He was bound to feel remorseful and no doubt make his children feel remorse for their frankness. Nor did he want it known, as she lay dying, that he was writing daily letters to women friends, Janet Stone in particular. His code allowed for tea and sympathy, but to name names, hurting those involved—such a man was no gent. I should have anticipated the objections coming from him, written in an increasingly shaky hand. I should have known that the most painful thought of all was that he was somehow responsible for Jane's predicament. Many observers told me that when K was away, Jane never touched a drop. Mr. Linley voiced the same comment one day. K looked at him and said, "You mean it's my fault then?"

He wanted far less emphasis placed on Jane's drinking and no asides from me about the possible reasons why, thank you very much. He wanted all of his letters to Janet removed. In other words, despite the agreement we had made about my editorial independence, he was dictating content and tone in exchange for my right to quote from his other letters—and his permission would be essential because of copyright laws protecting unpublished writings. I wasted a lot of time reminding him of our written agreement and getting him to change his mind. What I should have done was booked a flight on the next plane, mindful of Bernard Berenson's comment to an acolyte: "If you want something from me, come and see me personally because it's too easy to say no in a letter." As it was, with Alan and Nolwen hovering in the background, I was not about to walk into the lion's den. So I went into my study and rewrote for a month, acceding to his request as much as I could without compromising my principles. My husband practically left trays outside my door.

In the middle of all this, with nothing really settled, K died. He had finally needed the hip operation Nolwen had been agitating for. He seemed to recover, but then his heart failed in May 1983 at the age of seventy-nine. Alan Clark, his literary executor, took up the cudgel with zest. When there is a vacuum at the center, it is amazing how many people move in. Besides Alan, I counted Colette and Colin Clark, Nolwen Clark, Jock Murray, their agent, Maggie Hanbury, my agent, Murray Pollinger, my two London editors and my New York editor. It was censorship

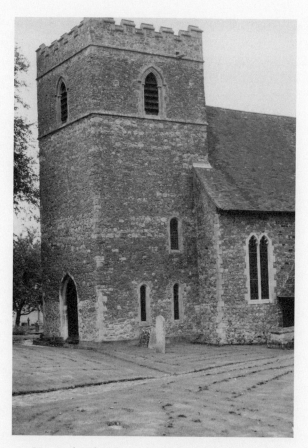

Kenneth Clark's grave in the grounds of the
parish church at Saltwood

by committee. The more I attempted to weave my way through
the individual objections, the more miscommunications, mis-
understandings and criticisms arose. What eventually emerged
was that, in exchange for the approval of direct quotes, the family wanted veto power over the revised manuscript. After a year's
battering I was in no mood to show them anything else. I told
them to go to hell.

Once this news sank in, Jock Murray withdrew as co-
publisher and presumably the Clarks got their money back. I
had further work to do on the manuscript, taking out the

remaining direct quotes and putting them into paraphrase. But it did remove the Clarks, their agent and their watchful editor, in one clean sweep of the board; Weidenfeld & Nicolson and Holt, Rinehart & Winston were free to go ahead. The big problem was that I had made an enemy of Alan, something I had been warned not to do. There was a letter from Alan saying it was a shame the book was so badly written, but he would save his "big guns" for the book's publication. I should have taken that remark far more seriously. Big guns there were. Reviewers fell on the book and tore it to shreds. Anthony Powell called it "uncomfortable K." Denys Sutton said the book "fastened on the warts." The *Times* of London headline for a review by David Pryce-Jones was "Through the Keyhole of a Top Person." The same paper quoted Alan Clark as calling me a 1936 housemaid. I didn't mind the housemaid part so much, but drew the line at 1936. Well, tinkerty tonk, as Bertie Wooster would say. What astounded me was that K's children, who had been all too ready with their parental criticisms, should have turned on me via their point man, Alan Clark. (I did not know how many of these attacks had been inspired by Alan Clark's string-pulling, but since he was now a well-known politician with friends on Fleet Street, I had my suspicions.) Peter Quennell was the only reviewer who seemed to have noticed the contradiction. He wrote, "meanwhile his elder son has denounced [the book] as 'tawdry . . . trashy . . . dreadfully banal,' though junior members of the family have contributed descriptions of his family life that are, to say the least of it, astonishingly candid." I was unprepared for the cool cynicism of the maneuver, and fastened on such crumbs of comfort as A. N. Wilson's kindly comment that the book was readable and interesting. There were much better notices in New York and elsewhere in the United States. Then there was the *Sunday Mirror*, which, because the book contained a reference to Kenneth Clark's passing flirtation with the Queen Mother, had the bright idea that this was the main theme. It published a lovely front-page banner headline: "Fury Over Book on Queen Mum." As John Curtis, my editor at Weidenfeld, remarked, it probably helped sell a few copies.

There is a great irony in all this. The diary Alan Clark published nine years later (1993) about his political career and private life turned out to be a compulsive spiller of beans on a scale that dwarfed my own modest revelations. In 1984 Clark told the *Sunday Mirror,* "I am thinking . . . about those persons alive today who may be embarrassed by what Miss Secrest has written." By 1993 he had forgotten all about sparing anybody's feelings, let alone those of his wife, as he gave a lip-smacking account of his sexual conquests (they had to be young and "succulent"), his abuse of old friends, opinions about politicians and all those beneath him on the social scale. Robert Harris wrote, "Clark emerges here as a thoroughly disagreeable character: a spoilt, devious, calculating, vindictive, boorish, vain, selfish, vulgar, faithless, pompous, whining dirty old man, with a sinister fondness for Adolf Hitler, or 'Wolf,' as he affectionately calls him. In publishing these diaries in his lifetime, Mr Clark has thrown caution, and just about everything else, to the winds. It makes for the most compelling account of modern politics I have ever read. But quite how Mr Clark is going to live with himself, let alone his wife and family and friends, is another matter."* But for every negative response there were ten other reviewers who loved his diary, and the volumes that followed, and him. The books sold and sold. He had inherited a fortune from his father; royalties made him richer than ever. The sales of mine were disappointing. That perceptive observer, the late Diana Menuhin,

---

* Alan Clark was Minister of State, Ministry of Defence, when he left politics in 1992. He returned in 1997 as MP for Kensington and Chelsea and died at Saltwood of a brain tumor in 1999.

thought the problem was that my biography was "too discreet and courteous" and that I was damned in some quarters for not "viciously exposing K," while still adding more information that "he in his skilfully slippery way slid past." She was probably right. The whole exercise taught me something useful, i.e., not to write about anyone I knew well, or at least choose more carefully. I was reminded of what Justin Kaplan, Mark Twain's biographer, called the first rule of biography: "Shoot the widow." Along with his literary executor, his publisher, his agent, his offspring and anyone else you can think of.

Chapter Three

B.B.

While I was still working as a cultural reporter for the *Washington Post,* one of the institutions I regularly covered was the National Gallery. This kind of writing, as with the interview assignment with Kenneth Clark, seldom had to do with reviews of shows, although I did make one or two timid forays in that direction when the paper's art critics were otherwise engaged. My job was to help publicize events, "flacking" we used to call it, and what was required was unquestioning acceptance if not actual gushing. So I believed that the late Bernard Berenson, expert on Italian Renaissance painting, was as hallowed an authority as everyone at the National Gallery seemed to think. Berenson's name was always invoked whenever the subject of a debatable attribution arose: "Well, B.B. said . . ." and that was the end of it. I would enter the great rotunda of the West Building, modeled on the Pantheon in Rome, with its coffered ceiling, its thirty-six-foot columns of Italian marble, and contemplate the bronze Mercury holding his caduceus above the huge stone fountain. I would stand in that vast echoing space if not with awe, then with a certain sense of intimidation. The weight and scale of all that stone—at one time the gallery, almost eight hundred feet long, covering eleven acres, was the

49

biggest marble building in the world—would make me acutely aware of my insignificance, measured against the power and authority of this temple to art.

I often met John Walker, only the second director of that institution (David Finley being the first, but, by then, immured in silence). Affability was Walker's most pronounced characteristic, along with an infectious laugh. This seemed admirable in the light of a serious illness in childhood; he had contracted polio and was left with a partially paralyzed leg. He would scad about that great space in a wheelchair, nodding and joking with the Top People, appreciative and deferential. I admired him even though, despite my unvarying attendance at press conferences and even the odd dinner or two, Walker never remembered my name and had a way of brushing me aside with the most dismissive of smiles. He had been one of the first to sit at Berenson's feet, and a whole host of "the wellborn attentives," as Kenneth Clark called them, followed his lead. Especially after World War II, Berenson had attained the kind of prominence that usually only accrues to elderly Japanese and rarely to art historians of any nationality. President Truman came to tea. Ernest Hemingway wrote him rambling, drunken letters and Jacqueline Kennedy came to pay homage at the Settignano villa he had bought outside Florence at the turn of the century and in which, over the decades, he had amassed a formidable library. His late diaries, *Rumor and Reflection* and *Sunset and Twilight,* added to the portrait of a cultural icon, one of his famous remarks being that he would like to stand at street corners begging people to drop their unused minutes into his hat. As a youth he had been handsome, with a poetic mop of curls. By the time he was in his eighties—he lived to be ninety-four—his great head seemed too small for his withered shoulders and fragile limbs; although entertaining constantly, he ate and drank almost nothing. It was always assumed he was in the eighteenth-century tradition of the gentleman scholar, independently wealthy, widely read, and without peer in his own specialty, which was connoisseurship.

Bernard Berenson with John Walker, director of the
National Gallery of Art

Besides Walker and Clark, other prominent acolytes were Sir
John Pope-Hennessy, who would become director of the British
Museum and later joined the Metropolitan Museum, and
J. Carter Brown, who succeeded Walker as director of the
National Gallery. Pupils, as I knew, were invariably bound by
inclination and reputation to their teachers. B.B. had particularly fancied Walker and wanted him to become first director of
the future study center he envisioned for his villa, "i Tatti." The
planned succession did not take place. Walker took the plum
position at the National Gallery instead. Quite right, too; but in
expiation, perhaps, Walker became Berenson's chief apologist.

Referring to the dinner hour, Walker wrote in his memoir,

"I Tatti," 1901

Self Portrait with Donors, "When I became a part of 'i Tatti,' I realized that Nicky (Berenson's secretary) and I were like stage managers of a production which required that one never permit a moment of silence. Always, the conversational ball must be kept in the air so B.B. could show his most brilliant strokes. It was fun, but it was tiring."

One of Kenneth Clark's endearing characteristics was that, polite as he was, and always ready to see the bright side, no one could accuse him of being reverential. His version of the same mealtime conversations went as follows: "The luncheons were very seldom harmonious, but this did not matter much, as most of the time was spent listening to Mr. Berenson. Sometimes two celebrated monologists, Ugo Ojetti and Carlo Placci, were allowed to come on and do short turns; and occasionally a rich old American lady . . . could contain herself no longer and would give us her impressions of Florence. . . . But in general Mr. Berenson talked without interruption, except for shouts of laughter and applause."

Even those who rebelled against the sycophantic atmosphere

of Berenson's court knew of his love for the natural world and considered it a redeeming characteristic. On one of his daily walks he was capable of looking at some familiar vista and exclaiming, "Where were my eyes yesterday?" He might pick up a pebble or an acorn or some beautiful weed, and bring it home to be displayed with all the pride of a precious ivory. His response to art was equally that of genuine rediscovery. One of Cecil Beaton's best photographs of Berenson came about when he followed B.B. into an art gallery and, from a particularly useful vantage point, caught Berenson as he stopped in front of a marble statue by Canova. The reclining nude was in the foreground and B.B., just behind it, was completely transfixed.

Listening to Mr. Berenson—it seemed as if I had been doing that all my life. It all started during my years at the City of Bath Girls' School. The school, on its own grounds in Oldfield Park, was housed in an ornate Victorian villa built by the improbably named William Duck, founder of Duck, Son & Pinker, which sold pianos and much else down in the town. It was the first truly grand house I had known. The entrance hall, in particular, with its broad, shallow flight of steps leading up to an Art Nouveau window of stained glass, its nobly proportioned hallways and air of stately calm, was an enchanted realm. Just to stand there gave one a feeling of peacefulness, and no matter how often I tore up and down that staircase in years to come, or queued up in the corridors leading from it, summoned by bells, as John Betjeman wrote, the entrance retained its serene atmosphere. Naturally the grammar school, which took bright kids at age eleven and kept them glued to their Greek, Latin and French for at least five years, soon ran out of space, so a graceless modern building was grafted onto the original house. Fortunately the local authorities had the wit to leave the grounds intact: the spacious terrace outside the billiards room that became our sixth-form room, the balustrades, the stone urns, the flights of steps leading down to the tennis courts, the paths that always smelled of matted leaves, the sweeping lawns with their majestic horse chestnut trees, and the sound that haunts them still, of a tennis game in progress, the sound Antonioni used so effectively in *Blow-Up*.

What had been the billiard room was a hexagonal structure with large windows opening onto walks and a flowered terrace reserved for the exclusive use of the two tiny sixth forms—perhaps no more than twenty girls. I used to spend a lot of time in the garden that was almost mine alone, and even when ostensibly at work, I had mastered the parlor trick of disappearing into landscapes, imagined or real. I discovered this for the first time during a particularly boring trigonometry class. To the left of the blackboard stood Miss Pugh, our formidable mathematics teacher. Slightly to her right hung a reproduction of one of Monet's series on haystacks. So, while ostensibly concentrating on her words, I was actually looking past her shoulder at the painting. Pretty soon I had slipped into the field and was relaxing in the golden light, inhaling the sweetish, prickly smell of drying hay. The class went by in a happy blur. I tried it again during French class one day in the billiards room, and did not return to my senses until the bell rang for the next period. The Arcadian vision that Bath exemplified had led to this: tactile values, as Mr. Berenson had it, and then some. From landscape to art was a short step. I was ready to be transported, and as my field of study for the Renaissance, I chose Italian art. I would prepare a lecture for the class.

My history teacher suggested I study the writings of Bernard Berenson, whose books were tucked away in remote corners of the school library. This was a large, untidy room, with parquet floors and quirkish corners that had been carved from the attic of the old building, plentifully supplied with window seats and chairs upholstered in a particularly harmonious blue. I had

Left: Schoolgirl, front of Westhill

Below: "The first truly grand house": the City of Bath Girls' School, 1961, with author in fore-ground

"Glued to their Greek": prizegiving at the City of Bath Girls'
School. Author in third row, fourth from left

already spent many an hour there lounging about, or curled up
on one of the window seats, gazing down over the town. Like the
terrace, it was a refuge and a reward, remote and secret. Pretty
soon I had memorized the main outlines of Berenson's aesthetic
and discovered Botticelli, Raphael, Giorgione and Giotto. Eventually I had prepared enough material for three lectures, and
gave them with gusto. This experience gave rise to the notion
that I had always known about B.B. and it never occurred to me
to question his status as ultimate authority.

Still, I had never thought of writing about him, and the idea
came about in a curious way. In 1974 I had published my first
biography, of the artist Romaine Brooks, *Between Me and Life*.
The book was successful enough—a review in the *New York
Times* by Anaïs Nin—to give me hope that it would sell in London. But despite the efforts of Doubleday, my publisher, nobody
wanted to publish it. Finally the Fine Art Society in New Bond
Street was persuaded to mount an exhibition of Romaine

Brooks's paintings. That led to an offer from Macdonald and Jane's, a house better known for its books about military history than the arts, and *Between Me and Life* was launched simultaneously with the exhibition in the winter of 1975–76. My publishers took me out to dinner afterwards and I met Francis King, novelist and essayist, who had not only recommended my book to them, but had written a pretty terrific review of it for the *Spectator*. At some point during the dinner the conversation got around to what I would write next. I was still working for the *Washington Post* and had not given particular thought to another book. But here I was, just remarried (a month before) and the subject of flattering interest from a publisher. My mind, unfortunately, was a blank. Then Francis King said, "Why don't you write about Berenson?"

I can't say that I particularly liked the idea. I had a mental image of a bearded sage, a bit like God, remote and inaccessible. But then Francis King went on to talk about what the cognoscenti in the art world knew, or in the London art world at least. That Berenson's façade of being an independently wealthy scholar was a sham. That he was a Jew from the Pale of Settlement who had emigrated to the slums of Boston. That he had worked his way up via scholarships to Boston Latin School and Harvard. That he had attracted the attention of a wealthy Bostonian, Isabella Stewart Gardner, and formed her collection of Italian Renaissance art. That he had subsequently changed sides and become an expert adviser to dealers, notably the great Joseph Duveen. That he had received twenty-five percent of the profits from a sale, a clear conflict of interest. That the word on the street was that at least some of his attributions were suspect. Francis King was sure there was a story there. Come to think of it, so was I.

As it turned out, London publishers were right not to jump at a book about an unknown artist. *Between Me and Life* sold nine hundred copies. Macdonald and Janes subsequently sent some stern letters that put the blame where it belonged, i.e., on me, for writing such a boring book. By the time that happened, however, I had jettisoned the airy preconceptions I had already formed about B.B., and was chasing the tempting thought that the art world would be turned on its head if it could be demonstrated that Berenson had indeed allowed profit to bias his scholarship. But first of all I needed to check Francis King's assertions with the one person I was sure would tell me the truth: Kenneth Clark. Armed with two new publishing contracts, from Holt, Rinehart & Winston in New York and Weidenfeld & Nicolson in London, I resigned from the *Washington Post* and went to visit him in May 1976.

By then I had read Berenson's autobiography, *Sketch for a Self-Portrait,* and was struck by the tone of remorse, of not having lived up to his potential, that pervaded its pages. How could that be explained? Lord Clark said, "Because he'd set out with such enormously high aims to become a second Goethe that nothing was going to be good enough for him. As it was, he had this unassailable reputation as a scholar and sage. He'd sit up in his chair at 'i Tatti' and people would motor up his narrow road and consult him like a Chinese oracle." "Ah, Berenson," an old Bostonian exclaimed to S. N. Behrman, who wrote a biography of Duveen, "he is so gifted that he might have become anything he liked. He could have been God—he chose to be Mephistopheles."

There was the further comment buried in Berenson's diaries: "You cannot touch pitch without being defiled." What did this often-voiced comment mean, unless it indicated some degree of guilt about his art-market dealings? Kenneth Clark said the rumors were true. Berenson was, "one can really only say between ourselves, corrupted." I should, he said, give much weight to the moment when B.B. switched his representation from the buyer to the seller. That pivotal date seemed to be 1906, when he accepted an invitation from Duveen to authenticate the

Hainauer collection and quickly became Duveen's expert on the Italian Renaissance. Of course I would need, he said casually, to work at the archives in "i Tatti," an extensive collection of letters and photographs that included a thirty-year correspondence with Duveen Brothers. Easier said than done. I remember one sunny spring morning in Florence when I made a phone call to Craig Hugh Smythe, then director of "i Tatti," now owned by Harvard University, from a box at the edge of the Piazza della Signoria. I was told that I could visit the photographic archives, but could not consult anything else. It seemed that, following Berenson's death in 1959, Ernest Samuels, an English professor, had been chosen by Nicky Mariano, Berenson's longtime assistant and mistress, to write the official life. Professor Samuels had been at work on his task since 1965. Until he finished—whenever that was—the archive was closed. Sorry about that.

I should have listened to Francis Steegmuller, expert on Flaubert and author of a prize-winning biography of Cocteau, whom I had met through my Romaine Brooks project—she had painted Cocteau—and Steegmuller's charming wife, the novelist Shirley Hazzard. Both of them urged me not to write about B.B. Steegmuller said he wouldn't touch the subject with "a ten-foot pole." I got a bit more desperate after I tried to consult the vast archive of Duveen Brothers, then under lock and key at the Metropolitan Museum, and was turned away there as well.

I would have given up at that point, had it not been for Kenneth Clark. At the moment when he was witnessing Jane's slow and inexorable decline, I was coming up with this interesting new idea. He was fascinated. He said, "It's the story about a youth of brilliant promise and idealism and marvelous gifts who didn't exactly sell himself, but hated rough living and got into this doubtful world. If only he had admitted, 'I didn't want to be poor!' From about 1906 to 1930 he lived in this world of power and people coming and sucking up to him, on their knees, literally. Max Friedländer, director of the Kaiser Friedrich Museum,

Bernard Berenson, Duveen's expert on the Italian Renaissance

would hold an audience once a week in an enormous room and all the dealers would sit with their pictures on their knees. Friedländer would go around the table and say, 'Hieronymus Bosch it isn't,' and that is what was happening to B.B. After the slump of 1929 he was less fussed over, and during World War II, when he had nothing to do but write, he began to recover and became infinitely sweeter and nicer. The drift away from the great world of attribution had begun. This brilliant young man might have lost his soul entirely and it looked jolly likely, but he hadn't." I should see the story, he said, as "the rise, and fall, and rise of a man." He added, "Shan't we have fun with your book!" That settled it.

If I couldn't consult the original material, what was I to do? Lord Clark advised me to see what Berenson was saying about a painting before he had a commercial interest in it, and then what he said about it once he was working for Duveen, but also for Wildenstein, Contini-Bonacossi and others. He was referring to the "Four Gospels," as they were called, the slim lists of paintings Berenson had published in the last years of the nineteenth century, giving his conclusions about who had painted what. B.B. had seen most of the paintings in European museums and churches, and been admitted to a few select private collections. I should compare those dates: *The Venetian Painters of the Renaissance,* 1894, the Florentine, 1896, the Central Italian, 1897, and the North Italian, 1907, with the attributions he gave once he went to work for Duveen. I knew without being told the huge gulf, in terms of price, separating even such innocent conclusions as "Bellini and Assistants" from the later pronouncement that the work was by the master alone. Tiny adjustments like this could bump up the price a hundredfold. Kenneth Clark made it sound so easy. All I had to do was find enough instances of paintings that suddenly shot up in B.B.'s estimation once he had a vested interest in the sale. Easier said than done. For example, the world is full of anonymous male sitters for portraits by Titian or for "Madonna and Child" paintings by Bellini that, in the days when paintings were seldom illustrated, and only differentiated by size and/or provenance (if you were lucky), just sorting through the confusion was full of booby traps and dead ends. Then there were the catalogues raisonnés, which told one everything if only one could figure out what it was. It took me a couple of years, but in the end I had come up with some respectable examples.

I was also discovering something else. My original motiva-

tion had been strictly journalistic and my research limited to
Berenson's business dealings. But the progression Kenneth Clark
had outlined, "the rise, and fall, and rise of a man," was too
intriguing to resist.

There was a further incentive to see Berenson's life in a larger
context. One of the people whose opinions I also respected was
Michael Gill, the BBC TV producer, with Peter Montagnon, of
Clark's *Civilisation* series. An investigation into Berenson's life
reminded him of an experiment in biography he had read years
before, *The Quest for Corvo* by A. J. A. Symons. I should read
this book because he was sure I would be intrigued by the
method and the parallels. That was all he said, but it was
enough.

Baron Corvo, alias Frederick William Rolfe, was a minor writer
of highly ornamented prose who had specialized in obscure literary byways and was best known for one novel, *Hadrian the Seventh*. This told the story of a candidate for the priesthood who
persisted in believing this was his mission in life, despite rejection by the Church, living in poverty, and with the bailiff at the
door. I knew about the novel because I had seen a play based on
it, written by Peter Luke and performed in London at the Mer-
maid Theatre in 1968. In the play, through a highly unlikely
chain of circumstances, the hero, belatedly recognized for his
years of suffering, becomes a priest and then the pope. As
Hadrian the Seventh he puts his Christian principles into practice. He thunders against temporal power, sells the Vatican's
treasures and gives the money to the poor, and institutes other
radical measures that immediately make him enemies. He is
assassinated (of course).

But back to the novel on which the play was based. Symons
wrote, "George Arthur Rose . . . sitting in his low, shabby bro-
cade armchair . . . who counts the split infinitives in the day's
newspaper as he dines on soup, haricot beans, and a baked

apple; who carefully preserves the ends of his cigarettes so that he may break them up and make a fresh cigarette when he has a sufficient quantity . . . whose garret windows are always open to the full; who exists in terrified anticipation of the postman's knock; this man starts to instant life in Fr. Rolfe's pages, for the best of all reasons (as I discovered later): because he is Fr. Rolfe himself."

Symons describes reading Rolfe's prose with increasing admiration. "I felt that interior stir with which we all recognize a transforming new experience." He is fired with enthusiasm for the idea of writing about this unjustly neglected writer whose chef d'oeuvre had been this warm and comforting fantasy as compensation for a life of rejection and deprivation. But there was more to be discovered. The collector of literary esoterica who had lent Symons his copy of *Hadrian the Seventh* also let him read a typescript of Rolfe's letters and telegrams, sent from Italy to a friend. Those letters made it clear that Rolfe was not only a pederast but was offering young boys for sale. Symons was shocked into anger and pity. "Pity; for behind the ugliness of their boasts and offers, these letters told a harrowing story of a man sliding desperately downhill, unable to pay for clothes, light or food; living like a rat in the bottom of an empty boat, slinking along side streets in misery at frustrated talents and missed chances, with no money in his pocket or meat in his belly, who had come at last to convince himself that every man's hand was against him."

This terrible and squalid end could hardly be compared with that of Berenson, praised, admired and courted in his beautiful villa on a hillside outside Florence. Yet there was the theme of appearance versus reality that was common to both. There was Fr. Rolfe (who abbreviated *Frederick* to make it look as if he had been ordained, and invented his Italian title) assuming a cloak of saintliness to hide the sordid truth. And there was Berenson, the poor boy from the Boston slums, who posed as a gentleman scholar, raging against the venality of a world in which he had all too willingly immersed himself. The result in both cases was colossal self-delusion.

As it happened, I knew something about constructing a false persona, because I had tried it myself. After World War II my parents and I emigrated to Canada on the old Cunard liner *Aquitania,* which was new when World War I began. It was a troop ship during the Second World War, and émigrés from Britain were housed in the vast dormitories that had held thousands of Canadian and American soldiers. I was just eighteen, violently seasick and scared.

We disembarked at Halifax, Nova Scotia, and boarded the train to take us to Hamilton, Ontario, where we were going to stay with my aunt Flo, on my mother's side, who had married a Canadian soldier during World War I and left Bath forever. To save space in the trunks, my mother made us wear our woolen suits and carry our overcoats, although it was August. This had not mattered too much when we were crossing the Atlantic. But on that endless train ride down through Nova Scotia, New Brunswick, the Gaspé Peninsula, Quebec and Ontario, dressed in our Scottish wool jackets and skirts, the sweat rolled down our legs and the clothes molded themselves to our backs. In the days before air conditioning and diesel engines, one either sweltered or opened the window and was immediately covered in soot and ashes. By the time we arrived in Hamilton, my white linen blouse had turned black. For two days and nights vast forests rolled past our window, interspersed by the occasional village, no more than a crossroads. Since actual platforms were a rarity, the train would shudder to a stop, it seemed in the middle of a street, and one jumped down from a perilous height onto the road. At night in our sleeping cars, the beds would sway, the curtains swing and the train would plunge into the darkness, its whistle sounding a wailing lament.

Olive Doman, mother, and author, emigrating
to Canada on the Cunard liner the *Aquitania*

The farther west one traveled, the stronger the feeling of dis-
orientation became, as if one were looking at life through the
wrong end of a very long telescope. I saw it so clearly one sunny
afternoon. Just as in the memorable train journey in David
Lean's film *Dr. Zhivago*, we were at the mercy of vast, inscrutable
forces. The train would halt, begin again, and then be shunted
back into a siding where it would stand for hours. After it drew
up beside an embankment one day, we all climbed out of our
carriages to get some air. People were walking up and down on
the grassy bank, exchanging rumors. We were leaving in ten
minutes. No, that was wrong; there had been an accident up the
line. We would be there for hours. So I sat and thought about
the lines from Keats with which I had prefaced my travel diary:
"Magic casements opening on the foam / Of perilous seas, in
faery lands forlorn." The awful finality of what I had done came
to me with full force. Forever afterwards, the long, drawn-out
whistle of a train seems to me, as it did to Thomas Wolfe,
unbearably sad.

By the time we met Aunt Flo, always called Aunt, she might

have only been in her sixties but seemed immensely old. She had some kind of childhood ailment that had curved her spine; while not exactly deformed, she had a marked stoop, which you noticed a lot at first but stopped seeing after a while. What you did notice was that she evidently had a chronic digestive problem because she would often grimace, dig an elbow in the direction of her stomach, and smile apologetically. Although she had by then lived in Hamilton for more than thirty years, she clung to the old customs. There was always a pot of tea brewing. The piano bench was full of sentimental songs of the Victorian music hall. She sent away for English magazines and belonged to the IODE (Imperial Order, Daughters of the Empire), similar to the DAR in every respect, including thinking.

The house on Cedar Avenue was one in a row of similar suburban villas, up and down the block, with identical front porches lining the sidewalks. Inside, all was dark, lace-curtained and quiet, with a proper parlor and crocheted doilies. Outside, especially during the endless Canadian summers, the cicadas would strike up their nocturnal overtures, and the moths and other night insects would gather in excited swarms, executing their dance of death under the streetlights. Then, up and down the block, the porches would begin to fill up with neighbors, raucously calling to each other from across the street and waving friendly bottles of beer. My aunt, who never drank anything stronger than tea, would make her little grunting noise, dig her ribs and try to smile.

The city in which I found myself was four times the size of Bath, with a population of about 250,000. There were signs to that effect at all the major intersections into the city, regularly updated with, one assumes, much Chamber of Commerce backslapping. It was situated beside Lake Ontario and had some pretty beaches, almost entirely deserted, because such prime locations had long since been commandeered by huge steel, iron and textile mills. Unskilled labor from all over central Europe came to work in these factories, presumably the reason for the self-congratulation. My first job was with the Canadian Bank of Commerce at the lower end of town (Sherman and Barton branch), whose customers could barely speak English and had never learned to write. I would desperately try to distinguish between the checks they signed with X's, as Annie Oakley sings in "Doin' What Comes Natur'lly." (But we cashed them just the same.)

Hamilton had no art gallery and no orchestra, but there was a university, laid out on a handsome campus. It had little effect on a city that was driven, vulgar and entirely caught up in something called Progress. That turned out to be drive-in movies, parking lots, wall-to-wall carpeting, central heating and pastel refrigerators. These were being praised by an actor named Ronald Reagan, who appeared on television as a spokesman for General Electric and always closed with the slogan "Progress Is Our Most Important Product." The idea that coloring a refrigerator pink could be called progressive struck me as ludicrous, and I turned a jaded eye on the culture that accepted such a concept. I did not want to consume conspicuously; I wanted to create. On the other hand, to do without seemed so alien to everyone else as to be faintly subversive. That first Christmas Day, lacking a car, we went for a walk in the snow. We kept being accosted by people in cars demanding to give us a lift.

I think my father must have talked before we left about the wonders of industrial production that Hamilton epitomized, but I was not paying attention. He had fought his way off the assembly line and, by dint of hard work at night school, became a tool and die maker for the Horstmann Gear Company in Bath. He wanted to become an architect, but was happy enough to call himself an engineer. Once we arrived in Ontario he was completely taken up by the miracles that hydroelectric power, which he had never seen before, embodied. He would pull up the car beside a generating plant and stare as if possessed, while Mother

"The great big engineering magnet":
Albert Doman, author's father

and I groaned in the back seat. I should have known he would shoot like a metal filing toward the great big engineering magnet that Hamilton represented. He got a job almost immediately, and my parents began to gather around them a circle of other English expatriates. During the long, lazy summer afternoons they would agree that Canada was a "go ahead" sort of place. My father would light a cigarette, raise a glass of beer and reply with feeling, "Too true!" As for my mother, who had lived her life in Bath, she made us change apartments nine times in five years because there was always something wrong. They were too big or too small, too near the street or too quiet. One never knew, and undoubtedly she did not either. She simply moved and my father, Albert Edward Doman, ever compliant, shouldered their bits of furniture and moved with her.

I see from my *Aquitania* diaries that my idea of a well-rounded meal was a heaping plate of spaghetti with a side order of mashed potatoes. I had never thought much about my figure, and in the prepubescent school uniforms we all wore—blouse, tie, skirt and socks—there hardly seemed any point in examining whatever shape the clothes were concealing. But once in Canada the awful truth about my voluptuous outlines, as reflected back from every corner of the culture via Sunday supplement cheesecake, exhortations to diet in women's magazines, Miss America swimsuit contests, and the use of sex to sell everything from chewing gum to dishwashers, got to me. There was something called 36-24-36, and if you did not have such measurements you might as well die. I was unhappy in Canada, and unhappiness made me eat. One evening I demolished a whole carton of Neapolitan ice cream. But then I had to face a barrage of pointed remarks from bank tellers at the Sherman and Barton branch. One girl finally said, "Isn't it strange—I'm so thin, and you're so fat." That did it. I was going on a diet out of self-preservation. There were ever so many ways of giving up the per-

On a permanent diet: author in a homemade dress
with John Daly, Canadian boyfriend

son you thought you were. Acquiring a Canadian accent for starters, if only to avoid the polite "How do you like it here?" for the ninety-ninth time. Learning to say "bobby pins" instead of "hairgrips" and "sidewalk" for "pavement," "cookies" for "biscuits," "sweaters" for "jumpers" and "dress" instead of "frock." To talk about my hope chest, wear blue jeans, drink Cokes, read the funnies and learn to ice-skate. With each small accommodation I felt my past, everything I loved and valued, almost my definition of myself, slipping away. What was replacing it I did not like.

I read and analyzed *The Quest for Corvo* until I knew whole paragraphs by heart. I was just as much influenced by the approach Symons employed. He described his own investigation month by month, and the way in which the rough outlines of his subject's life became gradually more detailed and revealing until, finally, he arrived at the heart of the matter. Like him, I must see the purpose of biography as not just to record but to reveal. Like him, I must balance my subject's weaknesses against his strengths; to emphasize one at the expense of the other seemed to deny the very essence of human nature in all its contradictory complexity.

In the spring of 1976 I wrote to my husband from London, "I do wish you could have seen K's (Kenneth Clark's) documentary on B.B. It was absolutely inspiring, because it gave such an immediate feeling for B.B.'s delight in, and love of, beauty; it put the emphasis in absolutely the right place and made one immediately respond in sympathy to that love. My great task will be to communicate that in words—*much* harder! But I can already get a feeling for the impressionistic outline: the beauty of the natural world to which the child is born; the dark Lithuanian forests; then the squalor of a Boston slum; then the young poet-pilgrim, interchangeably in love with Italy's landscape and its art, so as to make a forceful contrast with the later, spoilt, Doge-like B.B. for whom money became everything."

I was used to the pace of daily journalism, and tore into the project; in one three-week period I did thirty-four interviews. I knew enough to realize that the serendipitous pattern of investigation that Symons had described was unlikely to unravel itself quite so neatly in my case. I had started in Venice partly out of the superstitious belief that if I began there, where Corvo met his end, some part of his biographer's luck would rub off on me. And in fact that autumn of vanished tourists, in the rain and fog, with water on the Piazza San Marco lapping over one's ankles, it was easy enough to imagine Corvo, wet and huddled under some arch, or shivering in the hull of a boat.

But I had chosen my subjects more or less at random. The first, a retired diplomat, was gallant and amusing but could tell me nothing more than I would hear time and again, that is to say, people who met Berenson socially only saw the scintillating surface. I had hoped for better from Count Cini, a wealthy nonagenarian with a famous collection, but I had not counted on his extreme deafness. After a few shouted questions I gave up in despair. Finally there was a prominent Venetian socialite. I had spent time in Venice some years before doing interviews for an article I ended up not writing, about the fact that Venice was sinking. One prominent lady was on the committee to save Venice, and I suppose I had expected some sense of urgency in her remarks. Instead she was polite but strangely noncommittal and I realized she was bored. Whenever I asked a lengthy question, she would whip out her compact and subject her makeup to a leisurely examination. Her response was part of the reason for abandoning the project; naturally enough I put her name out of my mind as well as her face. On this particular visit to Venice I waited all day to meet the socialite, a wealthy Contessa, said to be close to the circle at "i Tatti," whose plane was delayed in Rome. I was finally summoned for a drink in her vast marble palazzo near the Salute. I began to ask questions about B.B. that seemed to bore her. Then she suddenly produced her compact and I realized why.

"Give us this day our daily idea," as B.B. would say, "and forgive us all those we thought yesterday." I naturally did better in Florence, where the circle of friends and acquaintances orbiting around "i Tatti" were observing my character at much closer quarters. Since he had died in 1959, some seventeen years later there were still old friends, many "unser einers" now in their seventies, who had known him for decades and, like Berenson, had somehow survived World War II. One of them was the Marchesa Serlupi, wife of the former ambassador of San Marino to the Vatican, who had used his tenuous diplomatic immunity to hide Berenson and Nicky Mariano at the height of the war. The Marchesa regaled me with stories about how difficult it was to keep Berenson, supposedly an Austrian count, and Nicky Mariano from blowing their cover by sending their laundry to "i Tatti" to be washed, gossiping unwisely with the servants, going for daily walks and speaking Italian with (in B.B.'s case) an atrocious American accent. As soon as the war ended, B.B. insisted on being taken to "i Tatti" and came back "looking like a wreck," the Marchesa said. The villa had been badly hit during the Allied bombardment, and his hostess thought the shock of seeing the damage had been too much for the octogenarian. "He went to bed without any supper and the next day had violent diarrhea. I didn't know how to stop it. We put him on grated apples and rice for three days."

After my two-hour interview with the Marchesa, I wrote, "I drive my rental car back down the long drive; it seems to get harder & harder. Arrive at gate (¼ mile). Have flat tire. Open trunk—no spare tire. Find old man in gate house—he has no English and I, no Italian. No phone at gate house. Too far to walk back. And so on. Finally get to a telephone. Call car rental & learn that Fiat spare tires are concealed UNDER false floor of trunk. Marchesa sends grandson, tall, young, exquisite manners, kisses my hand. Speaks perfect English. Does not know how to change wheel either. Old man replaces wheel. Crowd has gathered. I am 24-minute phenomenon. Give old man 5,000 lire. Cannot go back way I came because of one-way street. It is dark. Cannot read map. Am swallowed up in traffic. But need I go on?"

Most of the people I interviewed about B.B. were personages in their own right, and I learned how tricky it could be to ask questions about someone like Berenson when those being interviewed considered themselves equally famous or more so. I always sent a query letter. Most prominent people are unreachable by phone anyway, and in most cases I never even had a reply. But whenever I did, I could be sure that the famous friend was in a tolerant mood and ready to talk.

This turned out to be true of Igor Markevitch, the conductor and composer discovered by Diaghilev, who was, by then, in his eighties and living in Rome. He invited me to lunch at a chic restaurant, where he was bowed to and addressed as "Maestro" at every turn; by the time we reached our table I was properly impressed. Maestro Markevitch had fought in the Italian Resistance and lived at the *villino,* a satellite building on the grounds of "i Tatti" where special favorites were invited to stay indefinitely. In his case it was seven years, so he was particularly well placed to observe from a friendly but not uncritical distance. He recalled that he and the French poet Marie Laure de Noailles visited "i Tatti" in the 1930s and were shown a Madonna and Child, Berenson's prize possession, which he said was by Baldovinetti. Ten years later, on the same tour of the house, the painting was now a Domenico Veneziano. Markevitch objected, "But you said it was—" "Did I say that?" B.B. asked imperturbably. "Well, dear boy, in those days it *was* a Baldovinetti." He also told me about an incident that illustrated one of the ways Berenson went about burnishing his own legend. *Time* magazine had published a story that Berenson's watch was warmed before it was placed on his wrist because of the shock of the cold to his delicate system. When reminded of this, Markevitch laughed. "Oh yes," he said, "I made that up." He had been interviewed by an Italian journalist whose insistent questions about Berenson bored him, so he began to concoct fantastical stories that the journalist dutifully published. He told B.B., and they had a good laugh about it. We had a good laugh about the gullibility of journalists. That was that, or so it seemed. Some months later I interviewed Bertram Goldsmith, who had served as military governor of Florence and was among the first American soldiers to visit "i Tatti" after World War II. He said the fake warmed-watch story was true. "One afternoon a butler arrived carrying a red velvet cushion. On it was a white towel and on that towel was a warmed watch. We asked about it and Nicky Mariano explained, 'We never let him put his watch on, because of the shock of the cold against his arm.' "

Markevitch knew, of course, that Berenson's lifelong ambition had been to leave "i Tatti" and the magnificent library he had assembled to Harvard University, his alma mater, as a study center. Cyril Connolly quipped that Berenson had been "taken up to a high place and shown all the kingdoms of the earth, at which he replied, 'I accept—for the sake of the library,' and there was rejoicing in heaven."

Like most people, Connolly did not know, or paid no attention to the fact, that Berenson was Jewish. There was a reason for that, as I discovered. Part of the edifice Berenson erected for himself was that he was not. While reading his early letters to his patron, Isabella Stewart Gardner, I discovered what he had told her: they had common Scottish ancestors. He was so convincing about his Stewart connections that she felt free in her letters to reveal her marked anti-Semitism, and whatever resentment he felt he would have had to stomach. In fact, it was not generally known that he was Jewish until the war years, when he made common cause with the millions who were being swallowed up by the Holocaust.

The differences between Frederick Rolfe and Bernard Berenson are most evident in their final years. Rolfe died of a heart attack in Venice at the age of fifty-one, still intent on self-justification, still blaming the world for his self-imposed problems, paranoid and narcissistic. Berenson, to his final days, was wrapped up and possessed by the idea of giving "i Tatti" to Harvard. In his eyes, this decades-long ambition would justify and excuse whatever accommodations had been made to the venal world that made such a goal possible. That this was his passion is clear in the anecdote from the Marchesa Serlupi. What caused his near collapse after visiting "i Tatti" was not its ruined state but his wife's comment that she hoped he had now abandoned his foolish ambition. Rolfe died, still trying to be a superman; Berenson, as Kenneth Clark implied, gave up the impossible task with relief and people liked him the better for it. And he had removed the mask of the gentile enough to crack Yiddish jokes with Sir Isaiah Berlin, Sir Lewis Namier and others, although just how open he was willing to be is another question. He still liked to refer to "our Puritan forebears," to which Meyer Schapiro remarked ironically, "His ancestors were Rabbis on the *Mayflower*." Berlin wrote to the author Iris Origo, who had known Berenson almost all her life and had mixed feelings about him, "I had no idea he was *so* tortured about his Jewish blood or so filled with dislike of everything sweet and ideal—nor so sentimental, or so self-hating: a marvellously gifted, shrewd, epicurean, cynical, mocking, savage old Jew."

Origo wrote, "We know little about other people, and it is gradually borne in on us how little more we know about our-

Matthew Arnold's Scholar-Gypsy, with Nicky Mariano

selves." And yet there was a change in him. The times when she went on walks with B.B. and saw the same vistas with new eyes—"Where were my eyes yesterday?," as he would exclaim—are her most precious memories of him. If the theme of his self-portrait was an immense nostalgia for lost opportunities, in old age this had been replaced by an appreciation of life's "essential realities" when, he wrote, "all ambition spent and passion . . . stilled," he could return to that sense of ecstatic identification with nature that he had almost lost. I saw him as Matthew Arnold's Scholar-Gypsy, and empathized.

> On some mild pastoral slope
> Emerge, and resting on the moonlit pales

B.B.

Freshen thy flowers as in former years
With dew, or listen with enchanted ears
From the dark dingles, to the nightingales!

There is a coda to this story. As *Being Bernard Berenson* was going into print, I received an important lesson about creating the proper impression. For years I had sighed over photographs of Greenwich Village novelists in black turtlenecks and heavy silver jewelry, but somehow this sartorial approach never worked for me; I only managed to look wan and uncomfortable. We had been living in a small village in New Hampshire for a while and my wardrobe had dwindled to Birkenstock sandals, wool tights,

Bernard Berenson in old age

and earmuffs. Then I found out I was to give a sales presentation at a lunch being given for me by my British publisher, Lord Weidenfeld, in London. Drastic measures were called for.

I got out my sewing machine and whipped up a few new clothes. The blond linen suit (with the circle skirt) went well enough, but the teal silk blouse with a Russian collar never did fit properly, partly because I did not believe the pattern about all that fabric being needed for the sleeves, and I was wrong. I then poured a bottle of something over my hair which had the virtue of turning an assortment of streaky grays and whites into an approximation of its original brown. I also bought a capacious red wool cape, which I learned had also been chosen by Kitty Dukakis. I don't know whether the wife of the former governor of Massachusetts ever used hers for a blanket, as I still do occasionally. I presented myself at lunch in my newly invigorated hair color and homemade outfit and was looked over by the sales reps as I tried to convince them that there was a hot story in this life of an Italian Renaissance art historian. They seemed unpersuaded, which did not ruffle my host in the least. "It's a very big property, a very big property indeed," he boomed. His kind words echoed in my head as I crossed back over the Atlantic. And the hair idea still seemed to be working, so I applied another bottle. We had been invited to a cocktail party being given by a pleasant elderly couple with, as it transpired, very poor eyesight. Since I had not seen my husband for a while, we stood in a corner holding hands and gazing deeply into each other's eyes.

A few days later I was in the local IGA supermarket buying groceries when our dear friend John Hayward, whose ear for local gossip is sine qua non, rushed up and whisked me over to a corner of the supermarket. "Have you heard the latest?" he asked, scarcely able to suppress his amusement. "What?" I said. He said, "You and your husband got a divorce." "We did?" I said. "Oh yes," he replied. "You left him months ago and now he's married again." "Who is it?" I asked. "We don't know her name yet, but she's going to all the parties," he said. "She's a much younger woman. She's a writer too, you know."

There is a further sequel. My Guggenheim Fellowship was to write a life of Geoffrey Scott, one of the bright young men in the prewar Berenson circle. Scott was well known for his brilliant book *The Architecture of Humanism,* and in the end I did not write about him for lack of enough information. But at the time I thought it possible, and one of the people he had known pretty well—they'd had an affair—was the poet Vita Sackville-West. She was better known for her tempestuous romance with Violet Trefusis, while being married to Harold Nicolson, author, politician and diplomat. The story had recently been told in *Portrait of a Marriage* by one of their sons, Nigel, Lord Weidenfeld's silent partner in the publishing house that had taken my book. I had met the other son, Benedict, so I wangled an introduction to Nigel and was invited to Sissinghurst Castle. As it turned out, Nigel Nicolson was still smarting from the lash of criticism he had received in some quarters for "outing" his parents, notably from Rebecca West, and could not bring himself to let his mother—he called her Vita—be seen yet again in a poor light. But he let me read Scott's love letters, gave me lunch and dinner, and included the very great treat of giving me a bed for the night in the famous house. My notes remind me that we talked the whole time about love, which seemed appropriate under the circumstances.

Our interview got off to a frisky start. He wanted to know what I had written so far, so I told him.

"Oh, you've written about the 'i Tatti' circle, have you?" he asked. "I suppose you wrote a biography of Nicky Mariano?"

I said no, I had written about Berenson. He asked who had published my book in a kind of "I can't imagine who would" tone of voice.

It was an opening I couldn't resist. "You did," I said.

It's a Story

It was my mother's idea that I should work at a bank. I suppose she liked the thought of me sitting beside piles of money even if, given the salaries in those days, I would never actually get my hands on any. Hour after numbing hour I would enter figures into an adding machine, only to find that the numbers would not balance. This, in a bank, is tantamount to the news that the sky is falling. All work would stop in an effort to find my error, which would only be discovered long after closing time. I had transposed two numbers—again. I am sure everyone was as heartily glad to see me go as I was to leave. After all, I was going to be a writer. I was taking a typing course at night school and picked up a sketchy knowledge of shorthand because I had been told by the *Hamilton Spectator,* the ruling daily, that they would not hire me without these skills. Back I went, nine months later. I had my skills. They still did not want to hire me.

The situation looked bleak. But then my father came home from work one day to say that a pal of his had a son working for another Hamilton paper, and the son was leaving. There was a vacancy. The editor and I met at a lunch bar for coffee. Ronald W. J. Cocking was a short, plump, unhandsome man of thirty-one who had recently emigrated from London and was now in

Ronald W. J. Cocking, right, interviewing John Diefenbaker,
future prime minister of Canada

charge of the *Hamilton News*. It had a circulation of about
11,000, came out twice a week and there was a staff of about
four, including Cocking. Its prospects were not rosy, which did
not deter its editor. With a sweeping hand he gestured toward
the glowing future awaiting anyone, including me, who wanted
to become famous.

At the time I thought Cocking was lucky to have a job, but I
came to decide that the *Hamilton News* was lucky to have him.
During World War II he had been in the Royal Air Force, where
he became a specialist in navigation as well as a Fellow of the
Royal Meteorological Society. Afterwards he worked at Scotland
Yard in some capacity or other and wrote thrillers in his spare
time. When he could not get his books published in England, he

decided to try his luck in Canada, and had landed the editing job shortly before we met.

How much journalistic experience he had I don't know, but he was a fluent writer, with a grasp of what it took to put a small paper on the map. If the *Spectator* was too fat and comfortable to worry about the homeless, he would write about them. Human-interest stories, blatant insider politics, graft, tax fraud, police brutality: these were grist for his tireless mill. His instinct for page-one news was tempered by a basic caution. He took the quaint view that we should report both sides of an issue, which kept the paper out of trouble, and in any case it was too small to be worth suing. So he was left to snipe and badger, and his free-wheeling style and peripatetic interests gave the paper whatever distinction it had.

He usually arrived at the office late, and I came to know his moods. If he bounded up the stairs, slung his coat on the rack and bellowed "Good morning!" it would be a good day. If, on the other hand, he shuffled in, looked blank, and went into his office without a word, then I also knew what to expect and it usually involved me. A second or two later he would emerge, waving some story I had written, slap it down on my desk and call it sloppy. On the other hand, he might bring me someone else's story, call me a "cuddly bundle" and ask me to "jazz it up," and I'd know a front-page piece had fallen through again. I am reminded of the comment about Jean Cocteau that he was the life and death of any party because he couldn't stop talking. Particularly after a few drinks, Cocking's surprisingly deep and resonant voice identified him in any crowd, and his guffaw would silence a room. I knew he told off-color jokes, but never around me, and I'm not sure I would have appreciated the point anyway, that's how innocent I was. He was boisterous, irritable, dismissive and even obnoxious, but at the same time capable of tireless effort, skillful, astute and vulnerable to rejection. He boasted he could teach anyone to write in six months. One of Cocking's less admirable traits was a tendency to inflate his claims, but in this case he was right. He offered to pay me $2.50 more than I was making at the bank. Still, I hesitated. I lay on my bed and hashed it out with my mother. This was hardly the distinguished future I had in mind for myself. On the other hand, it was a job.

The *Hamilton News* moved to better quarters quite soon, but when I first arrived just after my nineteenth birthday, it was housed in what had been a corner store with two large display windows of plate glass. I had a hard time finding the editorial section. The whole floor was a composing room, and for a very good reason. The paper had been founded by the International Typographical Union after a strike at the *Spectator* when the printers were locked out. In retaliation the ITU set up an opposition paper, providing jobs for all its striking workers. So the floor was very well staffed, but unfortunately none of them could write, which was where we came in. They had provided us with a balcony, equipped with a couple of truly ancient Royals and the kind of phones that still had separate ear- and mouthpieces. There we worked as the linotype machines banged and hammered away below us and the air filled with the smell of burning metal and vaporized ink. Down below, at deadline, Freddie, the shop foreman, who was small, neat and tyrannical, would be spinning around like a demented top. And I was learning to write.

As the paper's so-called women's editor, I was responsible for four tabloid pages twice a week (it soon became three times a week), my first experience of the yawning maw that a newspaper's columns represent. As soon as I had put my pages to bed, I would go home and lie awake all night desperately trying to figure out what I was going to put in the next issue. Unlike bigger papers, where the volume of news is so enormous that the problem becomes knowing what to leave out, I never had any overset. I wrote everything. The ITU, with all those printers to support, had no money left over for the likes of us. So there were no wire services. There was no money for taxis; we went everywhere by bus. There was not even much money to have photographs. These had to be sent out, were expensive to engrave, and I had to beg and plead for a picture. "Jazz it up" and "dream it up" were Cocking's favorite phrases.

There is a reason why journalists traditionally began just out of high school and are being kicked out by the time they are forty, if they have not retired to old folks' homes by then. Journalism exploits the tireless energy of the young. When I married and joined the *Columbus* (Ohio) *Citizen*'s women's pages I worked, if possible, harder than ever. One other writer, the late Charlotte Curtis, and I were putting out two pages a day as well as an eight-to-twelve-page section on Sundays. But the worst aspect of the print shop office at the *Hamilton News* was the ink. It was everywhere: in our hair, on our eyelashes, all over our shoes and typewriter keys and under our fingernails. Meanwhile, I wrote and wrote. I felt like E. B. White, who was once adopted by a baby seagull that he fed every ten minutes around the clock and who still screamed at him accusingly every time he went by. So, like White, I fed my section the verbal equivalent of chicken gizzards, chopped with clams, angleworms and laying mash, which it gulped down and demanded more. Under this relentless pressure my style, such as it was, did not improve. In fact I was awful, but this did not matter much, as nobody read my work except, of course, my mother.

As a young reporter my biggest problem was asking people for money. Well, it wasn't money, but it might as well have been. Early in my stay at the *News*, Cocking sat me down, gave me a phone book and told me to call people up and ask them questions in the service of some story or other, I forget what. "What, you want me to ring up perfect strangers?!" I said in my hurt and outrage. "That's right," he said. So I did. Nowadays, reporters from big papers like the *New York Times* and the *Washington Post* command everyone's respectful attention. The reaction I would

At the *Hamilton News:* "Jazz it up and dream it up."

get was "The Hamilton *what?*" and the phone would be slammed down. I did not have as hard a time again until I left newspapers and started from scratch, trying to establish myself as a biographer. This reluctance to impose myself on others carried over to asking questions at conventions and cocktail parties. I found it excruciatingly difficult and never could think of anything to say. In self-defense I evolved a method of getting people to talk about themselves. Since this almost never failed, I would gratefully start taking notes.

I was, without realizing it, carrying on some venerable traditions. For instance, I was told to number the first page 11111, the next 22222, the third 33333 and so on, I forget why. I had to end each page with a paragraph. In the days when pages were distributed among different linotype operators and set in hot metal, one line at a time, this made sense. I was also taught to put "-30-" at the end of a piece, and I knew the reason once, but have forgotten. Most of all I was taught to talk about an article as a story. Quite where this tradition comes from I do not know, either. As the late Jim Waring, Catholic University's esteemed theatre director, used to say, "We call them shows because we are *showing* them something." Similarly, we called them stories because we were telling them something, hopefully as entertainingly as possible. I did not mind putting a story together, but I had terrible trouble recognizing a STORY. What was a STORY? Cocking, who taught me everything, could not teach me this. He would shrug, advise me to read more newspapers, say, "If dog bites man, it's not news. If man bites dog, it's news," and go away. I thought I saw his point, but it did not seem to apply to anything I was writing. So I blundered on, writing my nonstories. Then one day I happened to write about a school for handicapped children that had been started by parents because the school system would not accept their children. To my amazement, the article was cited by the mayor at the next meeting of the City Council as proof of a terrible injustice. Eureka! I had figured it out. This was a STORY.

There was another kind of injustice I could not have foreseen. I did not realize that the *Hamilton Spectator,* pro-business and right-wing, accurately reflected the general social climate. This could be summed up by the French premier Georges Pompidou's famous remark, *"Mes amis, enrichissez-vous."* When we first arrived, Hamilton had a real downtown, with late-nineteenth-century buildings built like battleships from flaming red brick and ornamented with towers, turrets and clocks. There was an imposing post office building, a handsome hotel, the Royal Connaught, a theatre, a city hall with an interior courtyard, cinemas, department stores, a bus terminal, a railway terminal, fancy restaurants and clanging, jangling streetcars. Most of the buildings were clustered around the intersection of King and James streets, which was ornamented with a sliver of parkland containing a stone fountain that was a source of civic pride. All this interfered with the city fathers' notions of progress. The first things to disappear were the streetcars and buses that moved

The glory days of Hamilton, Ontario: Ron Cocking,
making a public announcement on the town square.
Mayor Lloyd Jackson is at left, with hand in right pocket.

large numbers of people, in favor of one person per car, guaranteeing gridlock. Shortly afterwards, the post office was torn down. That quaintly antique vestige of slower, easier days, the city hall, with its ceiling fans and doors propped open by spittoons, went next, to be replaced by a steel-and-glass monstrosity that required the leveling of several streets. The railway terminal and office buildings went. So did Woolworth's, Kresge's, the Right House, Arliss Shoes and Calhoun's Drug Store, the little china shop where you bought imported Wedgwood and the Honey Dew café, where you drank coffee and listened to the jukebox. The large department stores got the message and relocated to the far fringes of the city in tawdry malls. Bedford Falls had turned into Pottersville, but unlike *It's a Wonderful Life,* this time it was not just George Bailey's bad dream. The Royal Connaught, a tattered ghost of its former self, has just closed. Shops and apartment buildings are boarded up along King and James streets, and all that is left of the downtown are bingo halls, tattoo parlors and an abandoned fountain.

What Hamilton needed was a crusading newspaper, which it never really got, although the *Hamilton News,* which would have been liberal and pro-union without the encouragement of the ITU, did its best. I picked up by osmosis the undercurrent of idealism expressed in the idea that newspapers could bring about change for the better by shining their light into dark corners. Besides, a succession of characters rolled through our office, adding their bulk to the general outsider feeling we all shared. When I first heard the expression "Tell my mother I'm a piano player in a whorehouse, but don't tell her I'm a newspaperman," it didn't surprise me. These professional drifters worked their way up and down the Niagara Peninsula, writing for hire. They were always beautiful stylists but probably had the newspaperman's secret vice, i.e., the bottle, and, from their raffish appearance, had slept in cheap hotels if not doorways. I have seen my favorite, Phil, sit at a typewriter hour after hour, bits of Band-Aid on the tips of his sore fingers, cigarette burns all over the linoleum, constructing an analysis of some hot political issue about which he was surprisingly knowledgeable.

These men never stayed long, but in the intervals they wanted to talk and would tell great stories. Frank, our copy editor, had worked on the old *New York Sun,* affecting a fedora with "Press" stuck in a stained hatband. He was always trying to change *so* to *thus* in my copy, to my rage. These were tales about the old days fighting Tammany Hall, about covering strikes when they got a bloodied nose or lost the hearing in one ear; I would listen, wide-eyed. They were invariably self-educated and well read. I owe whatever knowledge I have of Thornton Wilder, Sherwood Anderson, Theodore Dreiser and O. Henry to them.

They would disappear as silently as they came, but after we moved to proper offices on Jackson Street, some new staffers joined us. Freddie Cederberg was the sports editor, a very tall, very thin and very blond enthusiast with a beautiful wife, who was always the soul of good humor. He and Bruce Davenport, the general reporter, spent many a lunch hour comparing notes about their new fatherhood. Bruce was as dark as Freddie was fair, with a dimpled, deceptive smile. His favorite hymn, sung at top volume, was, "Jesus loves me, this I know / 'Cause the Bible tells me so; / I am Jesus' little man, / Yes by Jesus Christ I am," and Freddie would guffaw. Then Bruce would talk about his secret love, Hermann Hesse, the novels *Steppenwolf* and *The Glass Bead Game,* and insist that I educate myself. We all wrote very fast under deadline, drove each other mad by talking out our sentences, a habit I have still not broken, threw in inserts with aplomb, and "dreamed up" stories from nothing much. Hovering over us all and directing our every thought, indeed our lives, was the concept of the SCOOP. Scooping the *Spectator* was everything, and whenever we managed to accomplish this almost impossible feat we all went out and got drunk. It was exactly like Ben Hecht and Charles MacArthur's *Front Page;* every kind of dirty trick was allowed, even required, and although none of us stabbed little old ladies to get the scoop, we might have. And Alex Jennings, the charming, raffish, single-minded, cold-blooded editor of *Front Page,* was not too far removed from Ron Cocking, who goaded us, scolded us, guffawed, pulled his hair and actually, as I once saw him do, lay on the floor of the editorial department and cried tears of sheer frustration. I got the message: you hiked up your straight skirt and went to work, getting it fast and first.

I confess that I thought very little about the status of women in those unenlightened times; neither did I discover my particular métier as a writer. I turned out the predictable women's-magazine articles about the usual subjects: food, clothes, men, dieting, marriage, suntans, and men. I needed no encouragement to be fascinated by haute couture, and in the days when Canada had a healthy fashion industry, I considered it my journalistic duty to discourse learnedly on hemlines, accompanied, whenever I could get permission, by my amateur fashion drawings. Food was a different proposition. My mother had never trusted me with eggs, flour, sugar or milk, let alone meat, and my expertise as a cook was limited to onion soup, potato salad and grilled cheese sandwiches. But, as a writer, I had this insane kind of confidence. "How hard can it be?" I asked myself as I began a cooking column. I published a recipe for a cake using two and a half cups of flour. The next day I had a phone call from someone who was using the recipe. This surprised me. I was used to the idea that I wrote into a kind of void from which no one would emerge even if I printed the complete text of the Kama Sutra. What could I do to help this sterling reader? She was apologetic. It was just that she had thrown in her first fifteen cups of flour and the batter was getting awfully stiff. What should she do? Too late I realized that, thanks to a typographical error, what we had published was not two and a half cups of flour, but *twenty*-two and a half.

I never knew when I would be pressed into service to report on City Hall, a five-legged dog, a visiting dignitary or traffic court, the *News* having very little confidence in my ability to report on more serious derelictions. But even my willingness to try anything once was put to the test the day King George VI died, Wednesday, February 6, 1952. As it happened, a paper had been printed that morning, and when I went into the office at 9:00 a.m., Cocking was putting out a special edition. The paper having no wire service, he was writing all the stories himself. He had cleared the front page, set some banner headlines, put a black border around everything, and was typing the lead story from nonstop news reports coming across the radio, courtesy of the CBC and local stations. Because Princess Elizabeth and Prince Philip had visited the city only months before, it was particularly big news for Hamilton. Cocking sat me down at a rival program on another radio set, and together we began pounding out parallel stories that he eventually cut and pasted into one very long article marked "(Special)." It was special, all right. I'd never worked so hard in my life. We cleared the back page as well, and that was full of spin-off stories: Cabinet reacts, President Truman sends condolences, flags at half mast, that kind of thing. I then had the novel experience of standing outside the building selling newspapers, and they went like magic. It was amusing, to say the least, to see people willing to pay money for what they had just been hearing on the radio.

Unlike some editors, Ron Cocking never needed the stimulus of booze to start him writing. He lived, of course, on endless cups of coffee, but so did we all. He smoked nonstop, but that was also routine; I alone could not get the hang of it. After hours we all experimented with scotch, gin, bourbon, and rum, chased down with hamburgers and grilled cheeses. Those alcohol-drenched evenings were often dictated by the constant ups and downs of Cocking's love life. He was hopelessly enamored of Olivia, who lived somewhere in the American Deep South, an exotic concept to me then. He carried out his courtship on a battered Smith-Corona in a fast hunt-and-peck, two-fingered style, drumming a tattoo. These letters (as I knew, because he showed them to me) made up in poetic eloquence for what they lacked in presentation, being erratically spaced and full of errors. In those days, if your lines were not full of X'd-out copy, the preferred method being "zxzxzxzxzxzxzx," and festooned with ballooned phrases and frequent references to inserts A, B and C, then stuck together with a mushy glue that seeped through the pages and got on your fingers and clothes, you needn't bother to call yourself a journalist. Olivia wrote back just as spiritedly, if a lot more neatly. Once in a while I would be called in to referee, because she had dashed off something formal and cutting and it would turn out that this was in reply to something he had written, formal and cutting, and then forgotten about. On occasion things would look really bad, and that called for a whole evening of remorseful soul-searching. I remember once that several of us went on an evening boat trip and he stared out morosely over Lake Ontario, confessing his doubts about their future together and his whole existence as a human being. In fact the best thing would be if he just jumped and got it over with. I did not seriously think he would jump, but I was worried enough to keep him talking for two or three hours, and in the end he and Olivia were reconciled. I used to wonder what they were going to do, without me to explain them to each other. In fact they did get married, had a family, and later split up; but that's another story.

About the meanest trick I ever pulled on anyone I did to Ron Cocking, and it came about in a curious way. After Bruce Davenport decided to leave and make an honest living in advertising, we were joined by Lew Rodgers, a young Englishman. Like me, he had just arrived and his wardrobe was confined to one shiny gray suit with a faint stripe in it, and a matching waistcoat. If ever a boy looked marked for the musical stage, it was Lew. He was of average height, very slim, with a shock of slick brown hair, engaging features and a way of entering a room that had presence written all over it. You can't learn it; you are born with it. Perhaps he grew up in a trunk; he denied it, saying his father was a bookie. Perhaps he couldn't sing. I never heard him, but on the other hand we both liked to dance. He was light and rapid on his feet and swung me around the room as if I were straw. I got used to seeing him in his Dickensian outfit and did not notice that he was handsome until one day he turned up in a brand-new, head-turning ensemble and I realized what I had been missing. But by then I was engaged.

What Lew lacked in Bruce's devilishness and literary tastes, he made up for by means of clever plots that he used to try and drag me into. On one occasion he succeeded. Ron had just finished his third novel, *Weep No More, Lady,* a "dope thriller" it was called, about a young police reporter who gets himself into serious trouble with an international narcotics ring when he begins investigating the suspicious death of an elderly news dealer. Given Ron's usual messy delivery, the manuscript was almost illegible. Lew was a meticulous typist, which gave Ron his idea. He summoned Lew, on company time, to deliver a clean copy. Naturally, Lew resented this, but, as a newcomer, did not know how to decline the assignment. I saw him banging away every afternoon, and one day he told me the reason why. The exercise was extremely boring, but had become more interesting lately because he had figured out ways to rewrite the story. The police reporter hero was destined for several harrowing setbacks (kidnapping, beatings) from which he would always emerge because the author needed him to end up in one piece in the final paragraphs. Lew was busy killing him off by inches in the middle. He had also reworked the love theme so that instead of falling in love with the shapely daughter of the head of the dope syndicate, the police reporter was cuddling up to the ancient news dealer's toothless widow. It was all terrific fun, and to my eternal shame I joined in with a will. It took a while before Ron, absentminded as ever, noticed. Accustomed as we were to the spectacular scenes he could throw, we were astounded when he quietly withdrew the manuscript without a word. That was a story, too, in a way. We never wrote it.

Chapter Four

Metamorphosis of a Narcissus

If I hadn't learned the art of staring at a blank page from Ron Cocking at the *Hamilton News,* I doubt whether I would have ever tackled Salvador Dalí. Sometimes I get lucky and my editor will let me write about something that interests me passionately. In this case I wasn't even vaguely interested. I knew, of course, that Dalí was a genius at self-promotion, with his impossibly curving mustache, his deliberate massacre of the English language, and his ten-foot baguettes, but at the age of eighty, his best days seemed far behind him. What was left was "a seedy old conjuror," as John Richardson, Picasso's biographer, described him, "The Wizard of Was." I should have looked past the sequins and bad breath. I should have learned something from my study of Berenson. As it was, Dalí's name popped up in my life at a moment when my husband and I were both broke and the book business was going through a periodic slump. By now I was used to the idea that good subjects were one thing, and what a publisher could sell was something else entirely. So I was always coming up with suggestions on the hopeful theory that one or other of them would take. Thinking up your own projects is still a minor tributary in the world of daily journalism. Unless they have a regular beat, most reporters wait for the day's

Salvador Dalí

assignment and grumble later. I usually found that what a desk editor would pass on was likely to be boring. So, as taught by Cocking, I dreamed up my own. This trait turned out to be useful training in more ways than one.

But back to Dalí. It was 1984 and Jennifer Josephy, who had left Holt, Rinehart & Winston and moved to Dutton, had the nicest way of demurring, but she was saying no rather too often. Finally she said, "Think big." I knew what she meant. I went looking through the indexes of the art books in the house. The name of Salvador Dalí leaped out. Why not?

It is axiomatic that you don't write a book about someone if a biography is already in print, so my next task was to find out what was for sale. There were, as usual, plenty of Dalí picture books. There was an autobiography, almost certainly unreliable, but no biography. So I threw something together and whipped it off to New York and London. As luck would have it, Dalí had been in the news. All kinds of fake Dalí prints were surfacing in the art market. The rumor was that Dalí had somehow connived at this insult to his reputation, and biographies with a news peg are always at an advantage. I turned to my agent in London, Murray Pollinger, and in short order he obtained two contracts, one from Jennifer in New York and another from John Curtis at Weidenfeld & Nicolson in London. The idea was launched; the chase had started. I had no idea, echoing A. J. A. Symons, what an adventure it would turn out to be.

That I was ever likely to meet Dalí did not cross my mind. (In the end I did, but it was touch-and-go.) I was sure he would be well defended against nosy parkers like me. I envisioned a biography that would make use of the techniques I had learned. I would talk to everyone who knew him, on the theory that a rounded portrait must eventually emerge. There were other reasons why approaching Dalí himself would be a mistake. Two other biographers had encountered the great man's determination to control every aspect of his self-generated myth. Fleur Cowles's book took the view that Dalí was probably mad, and since this idea suited her subject very well, he cooperated. But before he would allow it to be published, every page of her manuscript had to bear his initials. Midway through his own conversations with Dalí, Carlton Lake made it clear that he wanted to come to his own conclusions; Dalí stopped talking. Tap-dancing around Kenneth Clark's heirs was too painfully vivid in my memory at that moment. I would rather have no access and write my own book. There was one final concern. I suspected, rightly as it turned out, that some people close to Dalí might want to be paid. That was something I had never done, and I was not about to start. So I would begin with no advantages. As I see it now, it was the maddest folly, but my mood was buoyant. I had two contracts. How hard can it be, I asked myself—as usual.

One of the first indications that there might be more to the story than met the eye came about when I met Alexander Eliot, former art critic for *Time* magazine, and his wife, Jane, through a mutual friend. He said their friendship with Dalí began in a curious way. On meeting Eliot for the second time, Dalí literally bolted. Jane Eliot then decided that Dalí really wanted to be invited to dinner, and she was right. The paradoxical behavior suggested by this seemingly minor incident nagged at my pre-conceptions. Perhaps Dalí's almost frantic striving for attention had created a smokescreen behind which a man was hiding, one very different and much more interesting than the image every-one knew. Then there was a painting, *Metamorphosis of Narcis-sus,* now at the Tate in London. In the background a figure, head bowed over one knee, is seated at the edge of a pool, raptly star-ing at his own reflection. In the foreground, mimicking the pose in an uncanny way, the thumb and forefinger of a right hand are balancing an egg from which sprouts a daffodil. The double image, Narcissus, the symbolism of a flower emerging from an egg—it all had the poetic and haunting nature of a dream whose significance one struggles to grasp. I began to look at his work with new respect. Whatever one thinks of his post-Surrealist style and his admiration for Ernest Meissonier and Adolphe William Bouguereau, champions of entrenched academicism, it was clear that, in the 1930s, Dalí was at the centre of Surrealism.

There were plenty of Dalí prints for sale in New York, and plenty of questions about the authenticity of the actual images, not to mention the authenticity of the signature. The situation was in such chaos that an expert at Christie's told me his auction house would accept nothing dated later than 1950. There was the same kind of disintegration of Dalí's reputation at work with respect to his most recent paintings, which, it was rumored, had almost all been painted by assistants since the artist himself had contracted Parkinson's disease. The implications of this news, given the extremely delicate attention to detail shown in Dalí's oeuvre, were serious, if true. In the 1970s it fell to John Richardson, then vice-president of M. Knoedler & Co., Dalí's New York dealer, to bring pressure on Dalí to live up to his contract, a one-man show of new work every two years. Enter Gala, the dragon lady wife, "one of the nastiest . . . a major modern artist ever saddled himself with," Richardson wrote. Whether Dalí was producing or not, she wanted money, endless quantities of money, which, it was rumored, were wadded up and thrust into briefcases that she, presumably, stored under beds. Born in Russia, Gala had once been beautiful. Now she, like her husband, was something of a joke, with her jet-black wig on which was pinned a Mickey Mouse bow, her pantsuits, her fur coats and spiderish smile. Seated next to her, Richardson would be assaulted by tiny elbows and fierce fists as she drove home her point: "Money! More money!" Not for nothing had André Breton concocted a famous anagram of Dalí's name, "Avida Dollars."

I sent my subject a letter and a book, a formality to which he, as I expected, did not respond. I did the same for Reynolds and Eleanor Morse, great Dalí collectors who had founded a museum in St. Petersburg, Florida. That overture was to have much better results. In the late summer of 1984 I took a flat in London near Ladbroke Square for six weeks, my stomach tying itself in the predictable knots while I waited for the first reviews of the Kenneth Clark book to roll in. I had plenty to divert my attention. One of the first interviews I did was with Eileen Agar, a tiny, bright-eyed member of the British Surrealist group in the

1930s. She was living at the top of a picturesque London flat, not at all claustrophobic, with all kinds of comfortable nooks and crannies, more or less dominated by a huge photograph of a smiling Picasso, quite nude, looking like some great big over-grown baby on a beach, playing in the sand. And she wore a brooch fashioned as a staring eye. Such vestiges of Surrealism were so arresting that I paid hardly any attention to what she said.

I also visited Edwin Mullins, a British art critic, novelist and television playwright, who met me in bare feet and sandals, jeans, and with a shirt open at the neckline, an outfit that would have been more comfortable on the Riviera than in London on a chilly gray day. He had interviewed Dalí twenty years before; it had been his first, and he'd been terrified. He went to Port Lligat, a small, sheltered, barren-looking cove not far from Cadaqués, where Dalí had built a house of white walls and terra-cotta roofs climbing up the side of a hill. "It was like going to Bluebeard's Castle," Mullins said. "I remember ringing the bell and shaking in my shoes. I didn't know what kind of a monster would appear."

Gala received him. She was neat and beautifully groomed, charming in a rather formal, efficient-secretary sort of way. She seemed to be the absolute figure of authority in the house, and very protective of her husband. Mullins remembered her saying, quite touchingly, that she hoped he was going to be nice to Dalí. As for the house, it was oddly comfortable despite its Surrealist mannerisms and the carefully calculated visual effect. He was taken into a completely circular room, surrounded by a padded banquette, called the "egg living room," and asked to wait. "Dalí will be with you." He waited and waited. The room, he found, had as many echoes as the whispering gallery at St. Paul's Cathedral. Then he began to hear the sounds of an approach, footsteps and deep breathing, but still there was no sign of Dalí: "I thought he'd never appear." Suddenly, there he was. "He had dressed up as a clown, a harlequin, a fool wearing a clown's bobble nose, a glittering, sequined robe, and a hat. In his right hand he carried a cane with a death's head and in his left, a tiny flag, the Stars and Stripes, which he was waving about."

Mullins continued, "I got the feeling he was sending himself up as well as living up to expectations. He was laughing at himself, just a little bit. He would strike attitudes, then look at me as if to say, 'How am I doing?'

"I found him a man of very great intelligence and knowledge. I got him talking about early photographs and daguerreotypes and he knew all sorts of things about them. He was very entertaining to talk to and among all the craziness of his views on art it was clear that, in certain areas, he was deeply serious, despite the exhibitionism."

They went to a party, crowded with young men and rich international-set girls wearing white stretch jeans, with a barbecue feast of rabbits, continuing their erudite conversation in a swimming pool. Mullins would have to keep climbing out to write it all down. Then they went to Dalí's studio and Mullins saw him at work. "He was painting a large male nude, The Apotheosis of something or other, and was halfway through the picture. There was William, a very beautiful young man who had been in jail, and I remember Dalí saying to Bob the Belgian photographer, 'It's important that we do not show him altogether nude or your paper won't publish it.' Dalí's solution was to hold a marl stick resting against the canvas in such a way that it acted as a cache-sexe. That was business. He never seemed neurotic at all. I thought he seemed extraordinarily matter-of-fact and practical." He liked Dalí very much, and, looking at the painter through Mullins's eyes, I began to like him too.

I was surprised to find so many people in London who knew Dalí, or knew about him, even whose mothers or fathers had attended the celebrated lecture in the New Burlington Galleries when Dalí had talked about Surrealism in a diving suit and then, when no one could figure out how to unscrew his helmet, had almost suffocated. Everyone seemed to know about Edward James, a well-to-do young Englishman from a prominent family who liked to claim he was the illegitimate grandson of Edward VII. At the age of twenty-one he inherited West Dean, a Jacobean house in Sussex, and Monkton House, a smaller shooting box on the Downs, along with a million pounds, and proceeded to spend it all on Surrealist works and particularly those of the youthful Dalí. Eventually he owned between forty and fifty of Dalí's best works, all painted in the 1930s.

Monkton House had been designed by Sir Edwin Lutyens and Sir Hugh Casson, who was hired by James to remodel it in 1936 or 1937, and who said, "James was an extremely elegant young man, dapper and small-boned, who wore shirts from Italy and ties from Paris. He was perfection." He also painted, wrote poetry, bought his first Brueghel when he was nineteen and had an impish sense of humor that coincided perfectly with Dalí's. At one time he owned a red sofa that Dalí had designed as a pair of pouting lips, and a telephone in the shape of a lobster. No doubt he never greeted his guests wearing a clown's bobble nose, but he did the next best thing. He engaged Dalí to turn his rather sober shooting box—not one of Lutyens's most imaginative efforts—into something rather more picturesque. Casson remembered the assignment very well.

"I was rather disapproving," he said. "I was this architect wanting to build a new world and improve society," and here was this Spanish trickster spending a fortune destroying a perfectly respectable house with all kinds of trompe-l'oeil features and sophomoric jokes. These began fairly mildly. Dalí wanted the chimneys to be covered with sculptured blankets superimposed with holes for the smoke. Casson said they could do that. He wanted bedsheets to appear to be hanging out of the windows. Some plaster ones were convincingly put in place. The tiled roof must be stripped and replaced with the dark green and black Italian pantiles that Dalí wanted. The downspouts would not do. Some iron columns, designed to look like bamboo, were about to be sold from the ballroom of a large house in Regents Park, built by Barbara Hutton, that was being demolished. Dalí wanted these as downspouts, with fake leaves added sprouting from their tops. Finally, an exquisite glass clock was mounted on the chimney wall. It showed not minutes and hours, but days of the week, each panel of glass a different color. Hand-tinted by Dalí, of course.

James was a great dog fancier, so either he or Dalí decided to remodel the interior in honor of his Great Dane. Stair carpeting was custom-made in pale brown with ascending, darker brown doggy footsteps. But the real issue was the living room decor, which Dalí wanted to resemble a dog's insides, complete with walls that expanded and contracted and the sound of labored breathing. To Casson the whole concept was baffling. As for Dalí, now that he had established himself as a successful Surrealist, he could be as silly as he liked and everyone would look for some kind of enigmatic meaning whether there was one, or not. The room was never made and the whole effort was a bit of a trial, even for Dalí. He complained to Casson, "It's difficult to shock the world every twenty-four hours."

Tim Heymann, agent for the Edward James Foundation, showed me through Monkton House, which retains many of its Dalinian features even though the glass clock no longer works, and such forays into furniture design as a Dalí chair shaped like two hands. Heymann said the two men fell out in later years, partly because James was such a dog lover and thought Dalí's attitude toward the animal kingdom insensitive if not cruel. But James kept, for decades, the pride of his collection, the *Metamorphosis of Narcissus*.

Ten days after I arrived in London, on August 31, 1984, there was a small paragraph in the papers. Dalí had been in a fire. Flames had broken out in his bedroom the night before, and he had suffered burns to his right leg. His doctor said they were minor. There was no explanation for the accident.

The fire took place in the castle of Pubol in a tiny village, La Pera, in Catalonia, a picturesque ruin that Dalí bought for Gala in the 1960s to compensate for the dream house in Tuscany that she wanted but never got. It was restored, with big rooms painted white, simple sober furniture and a few frisky Dalinian touches, such as doors meticulously painted in trompe l'oeil so as to fool the unwary into thinking they were open, and radiator covers to hide the unsightly radiators, cleverly painted to look like radiators—another Dalinian joke. After Gala died in the summer of 1982, Dalí took up residence in Pubol and refused to leave. He went on a hunger strike. He wanted to die. Two years later he had barely recovered, was still very thin and was being attended by nurses around the clock, so to have him burned in a fire was disturbing even if the burns were supposedly minor. What information there was, was being furnished by three old friends: Robert Descharnes, a French photographer and writer; Miguel Domènech, a lawyer, brother-in-law of a former Spanish prime minister; and Antonio Pitxot Soler, a Catalan artist. All three, it was said, had formed a wall around Dalí well before the accident. Edward James, for instance, had tried to visit Pubol and was turned away at the door; so were Reynolds and Eleanor Morse, who had built a whole museum around his art. None of his family were allowed to visit, including his sister, Ana Maria Dalí. And so on.

While I was waiting for my husband to join me on a trip to Spain, other articles appeared. It seemed Dalí was well enough to visit his *teatro museu* in Figueres, so-named, another large clue to the Dalí conundrum. Dressed in a smoking jacket and wearing a white turban, Dalí was transported on a stretcher the twenty-two miles to the museum in Figueres, where he inaugurated a memorial to Gala. Two hours after that, at around midnight, he was driven to Barcelona and entered the clinic of

Nuestra Señora del Pilar. It was just a precaution, his doctor said. But once there, Dalí's triumvirate could no longer keep his secrets, and the fact was that he was badly burned, on both upper legs, buttocks and groin, and his right arm. Burns covered eighteen percent of his body. If he did not have a skin-graft operation immediately, the burnt skin was threatening to turn septic; the doctors gave him forty-eight hours to live. Asked for his consent, and witnessed by a Barcelona notary summoned for the occasion, his lawyer, a photographer, and a reporter from Spain's national radio network, the painter gave a croak which was interpreted as *sí*. A team of six doctors immediately began to prepare for the delicate and lengthy undertaking. Plainclothes police stood outside the door of the artist's hospital room. Descharnes, Domènech and Pitxot moved into an adjoining suite. The hospital lobby was turned into a television studio and representatives of the clinic gave hourly reports. Dalí might die. And the Marqués de Dalí de Pubol was, with the death of Picasso, Spain's greatest living painter.

There was the further question of how the fire had started. The troika's explanation seemed innocent enough. There had been a short circuit in the electric bell Dalí used to summon his nurses. A spark had jumped back into the walls and these, since the castle was so old, contained saltpeter as insulating material, a highly combustible substance. Because the ceilings in the old rooms were so high, it took some time for the smoke to drift under Dalí's door and along the corridors. By the time that happened, there was a roaring fire and Dalí was on his hands and knees, crawling toward the door. Descharnes, a nurse and a civil guardsman rescued him and carried him to safety.

That was the explanation. As happens when people distrust the messenger, a whispering campaign started. It was said that the electric bell had made a tiny spark whenever he rang, and that Dalí had not had it repaired because he enjoyed playing with it in the privacy of his room. Was this the reason why his round-the-clock nurses simply ignored his constantly ringing bell? Was there any truth to the canard that the cause of the accident could be attributed to Dalí's well-known fondness for auto-eroticism? Was it the ringing of the bell, or the sudden silence, that finally roused the nurses? It was, said the newspaper *El País,* "a profoundly disagreeable mystery."

Behind the claims and counterclaims, the conflicting versions of events that seemed impossible to verify or disprove, was a further aspect to the Dalí affair. The value of the artist's personal collection of his work had been estimated at $78 million. Even though a sizable part of that, valued at $26 million, consisting of paintings, prints, drawings and *objets,* had been given by the painter to his *teatro museu* in Figueres, that still left the major portion, $52 million, in his hands. His will had not been published, and its eventual disposition was not known. Domènech stated that "all his personal collection will go to the people of Spain." What did this mean? Would Dalí's oeuvre stay in his native Catalonia, or would it end up in Madrid? One Catalan remarked, "There is too much money surrounding a lonely old man."

In the middle of these speculations, Isidor Bea, a Barcelona artist, claimed to have forged drawings, watercolors and oils with the permission of Dalí and his wife. The artist said he had been imitating artistic styles since childhood and had taken up Dalí's a decade before at the express request of Gala, because her husband's hand trembled so badly that he could no longer draw. This seemed to confirm the Parkinson's theory and cast considerable doubt on Dalí's claim that, between July 1981 and April 1983, less than two years, he had painted ninety-two canvases, or one a week. Even at the height of his powers, the best he could do was one a month. The assertion was made in October 1984, a couple of months after the accident, and by then Dalí was back on his feet. While conceding that Isidor Bea had helped him for years, Dalí insisted that the paintings were all his own. How good they were was something else. He unveiled a picture of a lurid purple beast, called *The Happy Horse,* and commented dryly, "I don't know if you can see that it is a horse or a donkey, but you can see that it is rotten."

"Too much has been going on behind the scenes," declared Pierre Argillet, a French art publisher and friend of Dalí's since the 1930s, who established his own Dalí museum at his château, Vaux le Penil, outside Paris. He said, "The trio of friends has put all others aside and kept Dalí's business affairs for themselves." Shortly afterwards, he and Descharnes came to blows in Barcelona's Hotel Ritz and, as luck would have it, in the presence of reporters. That was one I missed.

As soon as we arrived in Spain, I went to see the castle of Pubol in La Pera. I had expected a small village, but was amazed to see how medieval it was, not much more than a miniature square that was not even paved, smelling of manure and full of roosters, doves and old stone houses with slits for windows. One could hardly miss the castle, on a promontory, but there was not much to see from the other side of a high stone wall, and every window was shuttered. However, one could identify the fateful bedroom from the boarded-up window and stone that was blackened and charred.

The next stop was the clinic of Nuestra Señora del Pilar in Barcelona. I had tried to reach Dalí's command post by phone, but without success, so my husband and I decided to go there in person. We had the address and a badly printed street map that gave no more than a vague general indication of the hospital's whereabouts. We were driving down an avenue at a brisk pace when, out of the corner of my eye, I caught the words *Flores* and *Pilar.* "Stop!" I screamed; we had just shot past the hospital and an adjacent flower shop. It was so easy. There was a place to park on the street, and we simply walked in. If there were any TV cameras left we did not see them; the lobby had been reclaimed by the nuns, as nurses, and mothers with new babies. No one asked who we were as we took the elevator to the fourth floor. We stepped out. There was room 401, with Dalí's name on it, straight ahead. No sign of guards. Nothing. The door was closed. I had come all this way, and all I had to do was turn a handle. At that moment the most awful panic took hold of me. What if he was swathed in bandages? What if he was asleep? What if he yelled and sounded the alarm? We would be hustled out in short order. It's one of those moments you always regret. I turned away.

The visit did have the useful result of introducing me to Robert Descharnes, who had known Dalí for thirty years and was his chief spokesman and amanuensis. I found him sorting letters into neat piles, a short, stocky figure in his mid-fifties, wearing glasses, an open-necked shirt and the kind of expression one would expect of a man who had been harassed for weeks on end. Once I got to know him, I realized he not only knew what kind of a predicament Dalí was in, financially speaking, but how impossible it would be to get him out of it, assuming that Dalí even wanted to be saved. The business of the prints had ballooned out of anyone's control. There were myriad technicalities having to do with the kind of paper, how much control the artist exercised, how big a supposedly limited edition actually was, and of plates being reused without permission or acknowledgment, the usual ruses. The biggest problem stemmed from a practice Dalí had established before that seemed perfectly reasonable at the time. Since he traveled regularly between Spain, Paris and New York, after finishing a composition he always left behind enough signed blank pages to complete it. This worked to everyone's satisfaction for several years.

Then Dalí, or someone else, got the idea of selling his signature on a blank page. Why bother to create an image? All he had to do was sign a piece of paper—the going price was forty dollars. An eyewitness described the way it was done. Someone slid the paper under his pencil and someone else pulled it away, meaning he could sign every two seconds. Assuming he could keep this up for an hour, at the end Dalí would be seventy-two thousand dollars richer—easy money for an hour's work, and the signed pages would disappear into the underground art market.

There was a further refinement of this get-rich-quick scheme. Someone outside Dalí's circle got the bright idea of not bothering to use the artist at all. Why pay forty dollars when a perfectly good forgery could be had for half the price? The stage was set for floods of real prints with fake signatures, fake prints with real signatures, real with real, fake with fake, and such permutations in the hundreds of thousands. Martin Gordon, a respected New York authority, said, "There is not a great chance of getting a genuine Dalí, and if it were genuine, very few people could tell and I probably could not either." It was said that Dalí was too tired and ill to press charges and that even if he did, the suit might be ruinously expensive and inconclusive. Certainly the role he himself had played would have seriously weakened, if not destroyed, his case. Robert Descharnes said, "There is a lot of money involved. I never feel much like approaching the problem."

I knew what he meant. The combination of money and thuggery was enough to make the sturdiest art historian quail. When I was working on Berenson, who was known to have sold his opinions to some shady Italian art dealers as well as Duveen, the late Francis Haskell, professor of the history of art at Oxford University, would only meet me in Trafalgar Square. While we sat on some uncomfortable stone benches, the pigeons whirled overhead and he gave me words of advice. If I was going to start poking around in Berenson's business dealings, I had better watch my back, he said. After I started trying to make sense of Dalí's business dealings, I realized that I needed to talk to journalists who were already at work, in particular Alfons Quintà. Quintà was a former bureau chief for *El País,* who had explored the Dalinian labyrinth for years and was a particular expert on tax havens created for the artist by business associates such as Peter Moore and Enrique Sabater. Quintà, a former lawyer and policeman who had become a judge, met us for lunch at a restaurant in Barcelona. In Spain, we were used to having people show up an hour late and were surprised to find him waiting for us, seated at a table with his back to the wall. That he might be concerned about his own safety was evident and we admired the way, dressed in black leather, that he hopped onto his motorbike at the end of the lunch, donned his black visor and roared off down the street. I never felt in any particular danger, but that was probably because I didn't know enough. And I wasn't getting much further ahead.

Moore had a house in Cadaqués, and so did Pitxot; Sabater lived nearby in Port Lligat. It made sense to go there and at least try to get interviews, although I was not hopeful. And in fact we had to wait. Fortunately we made contact with Jean Levy, widow of Julien Levy, Dalí's first American dealer, who bought his seminal work, *The Persistence of Memory,* for the trade price of $250. His wife generously offered to let us stay in a house she had just bought in one of the streets radiating off the harbor. It was a former fisherman's cottage, with a door opening directly off the sidewalk, several small rooms and a spare but adequate kitchen. We discovered that our *piano nobile,* as it were, faced the windows of the houses opposite, which were almost close enough to touch. If anyone on the steep cobbled street had a party, we did too, in a manner of speaking. We were being swept up, willy-nilly, in the life of the neighborhood, at closer quarters than we would have liked.

This particular neighborhood was full of dogs and cats nobody wanted. I remember one thin, patient dog who lay motionless in the same place every day, waiting for his one meal.

That was provided by a widow living a few doors up. She had made feeding of strays her particular charity, and could be found at the butcher's shop each morning buying leftovers for her animals. The biggest group was a clutch of cats, half-wild and most of them thin and ill, who would slink down to the fishing boats pulled up on the beach in the hope of finding discarded fish heads and whatever else was thrown aside after the fish were gutted. We were walking on the beach one morning when we noticed a little kitten going up to a couple who were packing their suitcases in the back of a car. The kitten was meowing at them in the most winning way, but they acted as if it was not there and drove off. I watched its path as it retreated to a boat and crawled underneath in a small opening, prudent protection from the marauding German shepherds that roamed the village. This was a particularly pretty calico cat, marked with alternating blocks of red and black, with white paws, white whiskers and a band of white extending from its throat to its underbelly.

My husband was on instant alert. I have been known to pick up cats before. My son Martin and I once brought back a starving cat we had found on a window ledge in Venice and who enjoyed a modest fame after I wrote about him for the *Washington Post;* cat toys arrived in the mail for weeks. My husband was well aware of this fatal weakness of mine and was doing his best to explain all the reasons why we did not need one more problem at that particular moment. I wasn't listening. All I could see was this tiny little beast waiting under a boat with a kind of awful patience, the patience of the dog on the street and all the other starved and neglected animals. It was too much. I owed it to the kitten to respond to that mute appeal, or so I felt. I went back to the house to get a slice of ham and some water, and noticed that the kitchen contained a handsome straw basket with a sturdy lid. Back we went to the beach. The kitten was in the same place. It was wary, but its need for food was stronger. It approached the impromptu meal and began to eat. Then I saw something else: one of its eyes was completely closed, and yellow pus was bubbling out of it.

As soon as it was busy eating, we made our move. The kitten screamed and hissed, but it was too late. It was the work of a moment to throw it into the basket and secure the lid. Then we made our way back to the fisherman's house. I thought it was odd that our young captive, swinging between us inside the basket, was suddenly silent. When we got back, we found out why: it had fallen asleep. My husband did not know it yet, but we had a cat.

That stay in Cadaqués showed me the limitations of the quest for Dalí that I had so lightly undertaken six months before. True, a great deal had come to light, mostly about the blatant market in fakes, and there was more to the story, as I learned from Quintà, involving the labyrinthine international maneuverings Dalí and his associates had conducted in the rich man's pursuit of avoiding taxes, a goal so transparently routine nowadays as to be taken for the natural order of things. I could see, however, as my letters and phone calls from Cadaqués went unanswered, that my chances of uncovering more than had already been unearthed by Quintà and two or three other investigative journalists were about nil. Even so, the story I had pieced together gave the two sets of publishers' lawyers who read the book plenty of headaches. Peter Carter-Ruck, the British lawyer for Weidenfeld & Nicolson, raised almost sixty objections, concluding, "in view of the many references to manipulation, to fakes, to fraud, to excessive profit and to misrepresentation, this work necessarily contains much defamatory matter." Since I knew how easy it was to win an action for libel in Britain, I was at pains to comply. Even so, I was advised to put all our joint property in my husband's name in case I was sued, and also to take out an insurance policy. The only company that would accept such odds was Lloyd's of London. This venerable institution, I learned, would take on anybody, but the price was steep: five thousand pounds. Since this happened to be the size of my British advance, I gave up on that idea.

I was obsessed with the idea of meeting Dalí, but that seemed an equally bad bet. Descharnes, who spoke for the group, never actually turned me down. But he hedged the idea around with so many caveats that this, too, seemed to recede farther into the distance with every passing day. I was reminded of the maxim voiced by Hal Prince, Stephen Sondheim's producer, that if you can't get the right theatre dates and your leading lady comes down with pneumonia, maybe you shouldn't be doing the project in the first place. I was beginning to have this same superstitious feeling. The act of scooping up a pretty, abandoned and starving kitten contained a stubborn conviction that here, at least, I could do something constructive.

The one small grocery store in Cadaqués had nothing as exotic as cat food, so we stocked up on fish, raw liver and eggs. Our waif must have been someone's pet, because she turned out to have impeccable manners. She took to her improvised litter box (beach sand) immediately, ate with an appetite, allowed herself to be petted, and developed a mesmerizing purr. She curled up at the bottom of our bed each night and would still be there each morning, wide awake and politely waiting for us to lead the way to the kitchen.

Poucette, as we called her, urgently needed a vet, and we asked around. A visiting veterinarian came to the village once a week, on Thursday nights, and set up shop at an open bar on the beach. No appointment needed; you simply arrived and stood in a queue. We had visions of the kitten being lifted from the basket, taking one look at the parade of barking dogs behind her, and disappearing under the nearest boat. There had to be a better solution, and there was, in Rosas, where an actual veterinarian had regular office hours. We made our way over the mountains separating Cadaqués from the larger town and presented our problem child. She was in generally good health, he said, but would need some care from us in order to clear up her nasty eye infection. She was probably older than she looked, because of inadequate nutrition, perhaps a young adult. Then he told us about an American couple who visited the Costa Brava each summer and always traveled with their cat. They were from "*Cheee*-cago," he said, accenting the first syllable. It was curious, but . . . He shrugged. There was no accounting for Americans.

Day after day we treated the eye with the vet's antibiotic solution. The local hardware store had a seemingly endless supply of soft white towels, which we used as impromptu restraints to keep Poucette more or less in place as she squirmed and one of us aimed at the eye. Day after day she submitted to this assault. Then one morning, after the usual treatment, she suddenly leaped out of my arms, landing with a thump on the floor. She was momentarily dazed. But the news was good. Her eye was noticeably clearing, although it would always be smaller than the other. And she was getting better. After we brought her home, and for the short time that she was with us, she turned out to be the perfect traveler and ideal companion, alert, playful and affectionate, irresistible. In the end, letting her go was one of the hardest things I have ever had to do.

I had gone to Europe looking for one story and had come away with another, equally important but quite unexpected. Thanks to Joan Kropf, director of the Dalí Museum in St. Petersburg, I had been given the address of Gonzalo Serraclara de la Pompa, Dalí's second cousin, who had been his secretary after World War II and was, according to her, an honest man, the only one who did not exploit the connection. Serraclara had remained in the background and his name did not appear in the numbers of newspaper and magazine clippings of the postwar years. However, when members of Dalí's family, notably his sister, who had asked to visit him in hospital and were being turned away, Serraclara intervened successfully on their behalf. Perhaps Dalí's brush with death had inspired him to want to tell what he knew. At any rate, he agreed to see me.

His description of Dalí's childhood was a revelation. Dalí, son of a Salvador, was the second son to be named after his father. The first had died in childhood, and the painter was born exactly nine months later. The circumstances of the first Salvador's death, from meningitis, were never clear. It is believed that his father hit him on the head, and since meningitis followed shortly afterwards, the idea grew up that the blow to the head had caused the fatal brain inflammation. If true, there had to be some degree of guilt associated with Dalí senior's attitude toward his second son. His mother genuinely seems to have believed that he was a reincarnation of her dead Salvador, and that it was her role in life to guard him against the dangers to which the first had succumbed. That he, sleeping in the same bed, wearing the same clothes and playing with the same toys, grew up not knowing who he was, is evident. Having parents who, when they looked at you, saw someone else: such a dilemma has been studied. The more sensitive and gifted the child, the more impressionable he or she is, according to Alice Miller in *Prisoners of Childhood*. Such a child will grow up deeply insecure emotionally, even as he or she tries to play the expected role in a Pirandellesque fantasy. He or she may even lose contact with what he really thinks and feels; the mask will have become the face. Miller called such children narcissistically deprived and, by no accident, the theme of Narcissus is one that recurs in Dalí's work.

Added to this was the sexual insecurity Dalí felt and that his father appears to have exacerbated. Ana Maria Dalí said that her father bought a graphically illustrated book showing what happened to people with venereal diseases, and left it open on the piano. That, along with Catholic Church teachings about the

"A bulb in his head": Salvador Dalí with Gala at Cadaqués

dangers of masturbation, set in motion a series of taboos and aberrant sexual fantasies, ones that Dalí successfully exploited in a series of paintings of the 1930s. The more I looked, the more complex Dalí's story seemed to be and, at the same time, the more clues I was finding to his state of mind. D. H. Lawrence wrote that he was in favor of art, not for art's sake, but for his own sake. He added, "One sheds one's sickness in books, repeats and presents again one's emotions in order to master them." It seemed clear that repetitive images, ones for which Dalí became famous, and which inspired a whole vogue for his Surrealist landscapes in theatre, ballet and film, could be seen in a larger context, as the barely concealed compulsions of a deeply damaged personality. Then I found out what he had been thinking about when he painted the *Metamorphosis of Narcissus*.

The importance Dalí placed on this work can be deduced from the fact that he wrote an elaborate poem about it. In it he quotes a fisherman from Port Lligat: "What's wrong with that chap, glaring at himself all day long in his looking glass?" Another answers, "If you really want to know, he has a bulb in his head." Dalí explained that this Catalan phrase meant an illness, a complex. He concluded, "If a man has a bulb in his head, it might break into a flower at any moment. Narcissus!"

If, as Kenneth Clark has observed, "all artists have an obsessive central experience round which their art takes shape," then what was as the waves to Turner, the sky to Constable or the sun to Van Gogh was surely, in Dalí's case, the theme of the sea, or, more precisely, reflection. Just as Narcissus drowned himself while amorously attempting to embrace his own image, so Dalí, who had constructed a grandiose self to compensate for the freak he secretly believed himself to be, was expressing some deep truths about his state of mind in this perfectly realized, extraordinary painting. The bent form of Narcissus, half immersed in his pool of endless self-absorption, has, by a transmutation of genius, become the limestone sculpture of a hand. Between thumb and forefinger this mirror image holds something delicate, infinitely fragile and very beautiful: the flowering of his artistic gifts.

This, then, was the sad drama of his life: a troubled, brilliant man whose art barely concealed a cry for help. How often had he been exploited and, equally, acted against his own best interests? How ironic that his father had predicted, "You will die alone, ruined and betrayed." Narcissus, into what had he metamorphosed, with his melting watches, his ants, grasshoppers, crutches, distended breasts, skulls, boats, lions, eggs and, behind them, his barren, brooding landscapes? The double images, the hidden faces, the *methode paranoïaque,* memory's persistence— who bothered to unravel their significance nowadays?

By the spring of 1985, Dalí was well enough to give a couple of interviews with some of his old verve, and denied he had been walled off by his old friends. The fact was that he was ill and tired; he asked his friends to respect his privacy. It made the explanation of Ramón Guardiola, former mayor of Figueres, and others, that Dalí's vanity was at the root of his unwillingness to see visitors, very plausible. The issue was not that Dalí was prevented from seeing people, but that he preferred to risk hurting someone's feelings rather than face the humiliation of being seen in his present reduced state. He still had nurses and doctors in constant attendance, and was being fed through a nasal tube that made talking an effort. The explanation was that Dalí could not swallow, but no one knew whether this inability was physical or obscurely psychological. And he had abandoned Pubol, connected as it was with so many painful memories, to live next door to his *teatro museu,* which now absorbed his remaining energies. The building housing the museum had an interesting history. It was a former municipal theatre that had been in ruins since the Civil War—it had even been used as a fish market— and stood beside the church, San Pedro de Figueres, in which he had been baptized. He told an interviewer, "It's the sort of luck only I could have. Just to think that, at the end of the Civil War, a bomb should fall on the Municipal Theatre, turning it into what Marcel Duchamp called a 'ready-made.' " Dalí also called it a "kinetic Sainte Chapelle," adding, "Since everything about me is theatrical, I couldn't make a better choice."

The museum had outgrown its limited quarters and taken over an adjoining building that would eventually triple the exhibition space and add offices and gardens. There Dalí had taken up residence in what was renamed the Torre Galatea, part of which comprised the ancient ramparts of Figueres, made of stuccoed stone two feet thick. On one corner was a handsome circular tower, dating from medieval times. The building's interior, however, dated from about 1850. One entered a main doorway constantly attended by a sentry of the Guardia Civil into an inner courtyard, and mounted a stone staircase leading up to the main floor. What had been the principal salon, a room of handsome proportions with French doors leading out to a terrace, had been refurbished as the invalid's bedroom. Night tables and a bed, some chairs and a few pieces of furniture were arranged around walls painted with trompe-l'oeil paneling and fake marble. Carpets covered a floor tiled in black and white squares. There were another fourteen or fifteen rooms on this floor, and elsewhere one found a mélange of faded paper patterns in what might be Toile de Jouy, along with stenciled borders still bright after fifty years, high ceilings and, invariably, stone floors and fireplaces. Guarding the entrance to Dalí's bedroom was a nurses' station, with two nurses in constant attendance, and there a television set was installed, invariably showing a soccer match.

With the encouragement of Descharnes, I made a second trip to Figueres in the summer of 1985, convinced that another round of patient waiting was in store. Descharnes had warned me that Dalí could not be counted on, and was apt to cancel an appointment at a moment's notice. He was not going to talk about what I wanted, but only about what *he* wanted. He certainly would not discuss his family and childhood and would not talk at all if he thought I was writing a biography because "he is always sure someone will make money at his expense." In Figueres, a few kilometers from the French border, everyone was bilingual, and I had been interviewing often enough in French to suggest that I use it with Dalí. And Antonio Pitxot, the artist and old family friend who had, in many ways, assumed the role of reassuring and comforting presence once played by Gala, would be there to help with a word if necessary. As I expected, I waited for days. I could hardly believe the moment had come when Pitxot rang me to ask, with great cordiality, what time I would like to come the next evening to talk to Dalí, which really seemed to mean I would meet him at last.

As I went to the Torre Galatea, I could not suppress a mounting panic. Was he going to turn me away at the eleventh hour? Would I have made the trip for nothing and have to leave empty-handed? Conversely, if he did see me, how was I to deal with him, since his friends said one never knew what mood he would be in? What kinds of questions should I ask? The issues I most wanted to discuss were all those that had lain in the background for decades and to raise them would, most probably, meet with resistance. To see him and somehow antagonize him would be worse than not seeing him at all. A few moments after I had been ushered into the waiting room, I saw several men coming along the corridor, no doubt bureaucrats from Madrid, who, I was told, had appointments ahead of my own. Then his secretary appeared to announce that the great man wished to rest for half an hour before seeing me. I used the time to memorize an elaborate greeting in French in which I said he was doing me too much honor by receiving me. I really meant it, but the more I repeated it, so as not to forget a crucial word in the flurry of meeting him, the more insincere it sounded. By the time Dalí was ready to receive me, I was in no state to meet him.

He sat in his elegant, light, airy room, in a bedside chair covered in white. He was dressed in something white and flowing, white socks and sandals, his feet resting on a low footstool and his elbows on white slipcovers. He was at one end; I entered at the other, and although the distance was probably short, crossing the room seemed to take a long time. I was greeted by Pitxot and Descharnes, wearing a wide smile, who then left, and waved me to a seat on Dalí's right. I registered confused impressions of the famous mustache, once so elaborately clipped and waxed, now drooping and misshapen, white hair untidily pushed back and with straggling ends, his large, limp left hand resting against an almost grotesquely distended stomach and his right hand on the arm of the chair. A tube of horrible thickness jutted up into his left nostril. Perhaps it was flexible, but the rigid way in which it stood out, away from his body, conjured up nightmares about

the process of inserting it. Yet still more disquieting was the suspicion that even to have it in place was a kind of martyrdom.
Something about the stillness of that figure in the chair
telegraphed the impression that the only thing that gave him
strength to continue was his extraordinary willpower. Or was the
tube, perhaps, umbilical? It was difficult to decide because I was,
in effect, looking at a profile that betrayed not a flicker of emotion. As for his eyes, they stared straight ahead. It almost seemed
as if he were no longer alive.

I managed to stammer out my little speech, which was
received without comment and not even the ghost of a smile. I
wondered if he had heard me. Then I decided he had treated
that piece of gaucherie with the contempt it deserved. This was
most discouraging, but I persevered, handing him my little gift,
a miniature bird's nest, containing two minute china eggs. Even
that seemed inadequate, so I was not too surprised when Dalí
indicated with a marginal nod that he would open the package
later. Pitxot did his best to get Dalí talking. He mentioned the
Spanish national holiday of Santiago being celebrated that day,
which led him to Dalí's painting of 1957, *Santiago El Grande,* in
which a dominant motif was the scallop shell. This led to a reference to Botticelli's *Venus* and Aphrodite's birth in Crete and the
symbolisms implied. So many learned references would surely
elicit a reaction? Silence. I then brought up the subject of the
new monument to his name in Madrid that Dalí was being
asked to design. No response. A third subject, that of the art historian Kenneth Clark, whom Dalí had met in the 1930s, was
proposed, with the same lack of response. I was all too aware of
Guardiola's offhand comment, "If he doesn't answer your questions . . ." Whatever was I to do?

I plunged ahead. At last he began to speak, slowly, as if he
were gargling; I understood about every third word. The
museum, he said, should be seen as a single, immense Surrealist
object that, despite its apparent meaninglessness, contained a

hidden message. He alluded to Stefan Lupasco, a contemporary Romanian philosopher whose writings he much admired and who believed that extremes would meet in *la logique de la contra-diction*. He made brief references to future plans to expand the museum. He was still working on the design for a labyrinth. His answers were brief. If asked a question designed to elicit more than the usual stock response, he did not respond. I realized, by the way he banged the arm of the chair as he tried to concentrate, just how much effort was being expended for this particular performance.

I was ready to concede defeat when he suddenly volunteered something. "You know," he said, "I am a better writer than I am a painter." I was so relieved, I was ready to agree to anything, and for the first time he actually stole a glance in my direction. I had brought with me a borrowed copy of the poem he had written to accompany his *Metamorphosis of Narcissus* in 1937, that Julien Levy had published in New York. I also brought a photograph of Gala taken by Cecil Beaton, posed in front of two of Dalí's Magritte-inspired canvases, one in the shape of a male head and shoulders and the other of a female. Gala was seated, looking toward her right shoulder, one hand up to her forehead, her delicate wrist encircled by an exquisite bracelet, wearing a low-cut evening gown, the bodice of which seemed covered with tiny seashells. She looked pensive, and the graceful lift of her chin and expressiveness of her raised arm made one aware of her in a way that was difficult to describe; she seemed both remote and vulnerable. Pitxot held the photograph some distance from Dalí, and he looked at it without comment. Pitxot told me afterwards that it had been painful for Dalí to see Gala again. It reminded Pitxot of the time when, during his last venture into the outside world, Dalí's gaze had been directed toward an orange tree laden with exquisitely ripe fruit. Dalí had told Pitxot, "Do not show me things that I have loved so much and that hurt me so much because I know that I have to leave them soon." I had hoped to make a human contact, and had only succeeded in arousing painful memories. Unwittingly, I had done absolutely the wrong thing.

It was time to leave. Dalí kissed my hand, "a kiss in the air," and I walked toward the door. But I suddenly thought of the gift I had taken so much trouble to deliver, and wondered whether it might be overlooked. I turned to say, "Don't forget my present." At that moment I saw what I had despaired of seeing. His face was utterly changed. It was full, almost overwhelmed with emotion, and the appeal in his eyes was agonized.

Chapter Five

Romaine

I was standing at the bottom of the down escalator at Woodward & Lothrop's, then Washington's leading department store, trying to sell a book. Doubleday had just published my first biography, *Between Me and Life,* about Romaine Brooks, a neglected American artist who had been rediscovered by the Smithsonian Institution's National Collection of Fine Arts and given a handsome retrospective exhibition. It was the winter of 1974, and the perennial question, "Why are there no great women artists?" which, up to then, had always received the reply that women had no talent, was now being answered differently. Historically, women had never been given the opportunity. Now people like Rosa Bonheur and Frida Kahlo were being looked at with new respect, thanks to the women's movement. And Romaine Brooks was enjoying a minor vogue in Washington, partly because the exhibition had been so beautifully mounted. Her severely elegant portraits, in muted grays, black and white, displayed in wide gold and silver frames of distressed wood, in rooms filled with masses of white azaleas in copper planters, and her haunting Beardsleyesque drawings, were a sensation. The most striking painting in the exhibition was a self-portrait in black, with a mannish hat, standing in front of what looked like a ruined landscape.

Romaine Brooks on Capri in the 1920s

Now here I was in a department store, behind a table piled with books, learning what every author knows, that it isn't enough to have written; you have to know how to sell. And I did not have a clue.

I was sure everyone would be interested in Romaine Brooks if only I could get the story across. When one writes for a newspaper, there is a captive audience and one can therefore bring obscure personalities to the reader's attention whether said reader wants to hear about it or not. I had not yet realized that in publishing, it is the other way around. People would refuse to lay down what was then the handsome sum of $12.50 to read about some artist they had never heard of. Here I was, trying to sell the story of her life to one woman at a time—it was always a woman—as she drifted by, either not seeing me at all, or regarding me with suspicion. I knew enough not to pounce just because somebody had picked up a book. But when she asked who this person was, I knew I had only ten seconds to make the sale: "Themostfascinatingartist . . . Paris . . . turnofthecentury . . . motherwasmad . . . ProustColetteValéry . . ." It was discouraging, because there was so much to say. Hilton Kramer wrote, "Imagine if you can, a novel on which Henry James has collaborated with James Purdy, and you might begin to have the vaguest glimmer of the drama that was traced in the extraordinary life of Romaine Brooks."

Romaine Brooks had written an autobiography, *No Pleasant Memories,* in which she told the story of her young years. Her father was an alcoholic who vanished shortly after she was born. Her mother, a wealthy Philadelphian, was mentally unstable. She spent her life traveling around Europe with a retinue of servants and trunks full of clothes and jewelry, trailing two daughters and a son along with her. Her son, given the curious name of St. Mar, was a schizophrenic and dangerous, adored and placated by his mother. Romaine, the last born—she was so called because her mother happened to be in Rome at the time—was ignored and ill-treated. Her mother actually abandoned her with a New York washerwoman when she was six, in a slum from which she was rescued, like a Dickensian hero, by her wealthy Philadelphia relatives. Romaine left home as soon as she could, studying painting in Paris and moving to Capri, where she lived in picturesque poverty. There she joined an interesting circle that included the young Somerset Maugham, Axel Munthe, E. F. Benson and a friend of his, a young Englishman named John Ellingham Brooks. When Romaine's mother died, making her the heir to a fortune, she moved to Tite Street in London and, influenced by Whistler, a near neighbor, began to develop her monochromatic palette.

From the first, her interest was in portraiture and her sitters the titled, famous, elegantly scandalous and intellectually elite:

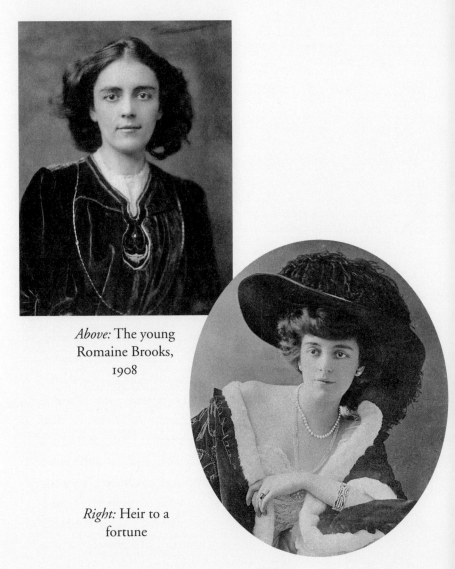

Above: The young
Romaine Brooks,
1908

Right: Heir to a
fortune

the author Paul Morand, poet Jean Cocteau, pianist Renatta
Borgatti, Una, Lady Troubridge, lover of Radclyffe Hall, and
Gabriele d'Annunzio, Italian poet and war hero. In 1909 she
exhibited at the Galeries Durand-Ruel, which, that same year,
showed Manet, Monet, Cézanne, Renoir and Mary Cassatt, and
was launched as a serious artist. She had married John Brooks as

John Ellingham Brooks

a matter of social camouflage, like most lesbians of her generation, but soon left him. She moved to Paris and met the love of
her life, Natalie Barney. Barney was also an expatriate, with a
modest gift for aphoristic writing and a talent for gathering
around her a circle of French and American literati that matched
Gertrude Stein's—and this circle was entirely unknown. It was
this world, or half-world, as Cecil Beaton called it, that interested me. I had been trying to write a novel, and Romaine's life
was so distinctive and bizarre that Doubleday actually thought it
should be fictionalized. (I managed to dissuade them of this.)
Brooks had lived most of her life in Europe; I had traveled in the
opposite direction. She had been an unwanted child, with a difficult relationship with her mother; so had I. I thought I was
meant to write this book.

One of the first things I learned was to talk to everyone. Most
people will know the obvious facts about your character and that
is all. They will give you a garbled version of a certain story. It

doesn't matter. The point of the exercise is to hear the tale told over and over again until the outlines are as familiar as your own hand and you are alert to the nuances and variations that will appear along the way. You want to meet the person who sees beneath the surface, and the surface was certainly arresting enough: the mannish clothes, the neutral palette, the gift for interior decor, the numerous love affairs, the jealousies, the wit and, most of all, the early experiences. She had tried in vain to have *No Pleasant Memories* published, and it was an almost unbelievable tale of childish terror and adolescent suffering, along with a heroic effort not to be overwhelmed by life. The portrait of herself as helpless victim, if not martyr—she compared herself with Saint Sebastian—recurs in her paintings, drawings and writings. Could she have been quite as persecuted as she would have people believe? Her friends, alternately sympathetic or disbelieving, gave me conflicting opinions. I tended to believe Bryher, the writer who had known Romaine for fifty years; she stressed the effect on the painter of being thrown into the constant company of her insane brother. "She had a very fine character but how she survived her childhood, I don't know. Because she could have been literally killed by her brother. . . . Romaine was saved by this concentration on her art," she said. "It was her only means of escape and if she hadn't had it, I don't know what she would have done. I was helping with mad people during World War I and it's about the worst case I ever saw."

I learned how baffling the whole venture to trace someone else's life can be. A voyage is a poor metaphor; the inference is a straight line, and this one went off in tangents in every direction. When I was still covering the White House for the *Washington Post,* Ron Hall, an English editor friend of mine, who saw me at work, said, "Why don't you write less and think more?" This was marginally useful advice for someone facing a daily deadline, but once I began working on a book his words resounded in my ears. I found myself examining every scrap of information, looking at it this way and that, for a hidden meaning. There was no logical progression, no step-by-step unveiling of the story. It was as if the tapestry of her life were being mapped out in tiny, unrelated sections of the canvas. Certain bright colors had been laid down, but their curious juxtapositions had not, so far, formed a coherent design. On the other hand, I was gaining insights in the most unexpected places. Just as I was writing an outline for the biography in which I stated that there seemed no reason why Romaine had married John Brooks, a letter arrived from Bryher. She wrote, "People seem to be astonished at her marriage, but I believe I have the key to that puzzle." Bit by bit I was assembling a formidable circle of new acquaintances in the French and British literary worlds, and since Romaine had only recently died at the great age of ninety-six, their memories were still vivid. They could be intimidating at first, particularly in Paris. I had to write letters with the correct forms of address. I had to wait for replies. I made telephone dates the way the French expect them, that is, at eight o'clock in the morning. Then one made a date for a second call during which one might finally be given an appointment for an interview. This rule was unvarying then; e-mail may have changed things, though I wonder how much. It was all very cumbersome but, on the other hand, one knew that if one had been given a date, they were willing to talk. I polished up my French. Almost the first word that rolled off my tongue was *prêter,* to lend, and I intended to carry off whatever I could lay my hands on. I learned to arrive on time, wear my very best outfit, smile a lot, agree with everything, always take flowers and follow up with cascades of thanks. The latter sometimes took an effort of the imagination, but the method worked.

Natalie Barney was, by then, in her nineties and living at the Hotel Meurice on the Right Bank with a companion, Janine Lahovary. Miss Barney had been a real beauty in her youth, with a mass of golden hair, and eyes, her friend Bettina Bergery said, "as blue as gas jets." By the time I met her, Miss Barney was a tiny little porcelain figure cocooned in white, her hair gathered up puffily at the back with a big white bow. She sat there quietly. In contrast to Romaine, who was an animated talker, Miss Barney hesitated over her words, and smiles of inner amusement played around her mouth. Someone observed that Natalie was feminine and analytical where Romaine was masculine and emotional, the kind of observation one would only get from the French. Another called her droll, *méchante.* "Everything she said was remarkable, original and pointed," and so it seemed. One of her memorable quotes was, "In England nothing is for women—not even the men." Madame Bergery said that the first time she went to a party of Natalie's at 20 rue Jacob, on the Left Bank, she met the French writer André Germain, whom Natalie had already immortalized in her Temple d'Amitié, a kind of classical conceit in the garden of her house. A statue had been erected in his honor and a tomb prepared for his eventual use. Mme Bergery said, "André Germain was a wicked little vest-pocket Voltaire. Natalie used to say of the tomb, 'Inside is André Germain, *plus petit que nature* [smaller than nature].' "

Bettina Bergery was speaking of Natalie's Friday-afternoon receptions, which she held for decades and which became as famous in Paris as those of Gertrude Stein. Mme Bergery was a faithful visitor, and her eye was sharp and unerring. An American, she went to live in Paris, took a job with Schiaparelli, the famous fashion designer, and "galloped around and went to parties." She married Gaston Bergery, a radical socialist and head of the *Front Commun* before World War II. By the time I met them, Gaston Bergery was stooped and vague. He took to wandering around the streets of Paris, and the police would have to find him and bring him back. I sat beside him one afternoon. My finger was bandaged and the wound beneath seemed to mesmerize him. Finally he took the finger in his strong grasp and was peeling off the bandage when his wife rapped out "Gaston!"

In her role as nurse, she was stoic and imperturbable. She had a repertoire of chic little black dresses, worn with perfect scarves and jewelry, and whenever she described the social scene, it was with irresistible animation.

Natalie's affairs, Bettina Bergery said, always had a certain style about them that was very much part of her period. "Natalie liked women with Greek dresses and crystal harps. The whole tone of life was very ecstatic in those days. Always to be in love with someone was a way of talking. Natalie also liked (besides Romaine) the Duchesse de Clermont-Tonnerre and Dolly Wilde. There were ever so many people Natalie liked. Natalie was a Don Juan, rather extrovert, rather frivolous." Whereas Romaine "had charm, you see. Very austere. A physical charm like that, and a sweet smile. A very warm, feminine voice. There was a moment in her life when she looked like Picasso, the same nose and chin and the same 'pistol eyes.' It was very difficult not to like Romaine because, as I said, she had charm. . . . I used to see Picasso during his Dora Mar period. . . . An abominable man. There were lots of ways in which he was like Romaine; the reflexes and defenses she had were so like him. Then he had lovely little seed-pearl teeth and his eyes could be so soft, and then they could look like pistol shots. Like an animal that can't resist making cat scratches. Romaine was the same way."

Romaine detested Janine Lahovary, the wife of a Romanian diplomat, who had met Natalie Barney on a park bench some fifteen years before. She arrived in Natalie's life and took over. Janine Lahovary was a curious choice for a woman with such a Bohemian past: exquisitely if conventionally dressed, with all sorts of French dressmaker details like matching edging and bows, expensive, highly polished shoes, and matching handbags, gloves and hats that she wore to afternoon teas. By the time she showed me a watercolor, hanging on the wall of their hotel rooms, that illustrated one of the techniques of lesbian love, I had built up an image of her and it was quite a shock. We used to take long walks in the Tuileries. She had a way of being gently confiding, minimizing Romaine's intense dislike of her, putting it down to Romaine's antisocialism. With great artistry she was painting a somber portrait of a dislikable old lady, small and cramped and twisted. That was when I realized that I liked Romaine Brooks very much.

I gained further insights into Romaine Brooks's life when I went to visit her remaining family in Nice, where she had lived at the end of her life. Her memoirs omit her older sister, Maya, who first married an Englishman and then Emilio, the Comte de Valbranca, an Italian nobleman connected with the Portuguese court. He turned out to be a tyrant who took over her fortune and refused to give her money; if she wanted something, she had to sell her jewels. She had two daughters. One of them, Béatrice, married Léon-Marie Emanuel, a distinguished lawyer. When I met him in Nice, Maître Emanuel was a widower in his seventies. He spent part of his year in a vast apartment and part of it in the picturesque Château de Manlèche, which I never saw, but he gave me a postcard photograph of it. His daughter Monique was married to Philippe Grossin, also a lawyer; they had two young children. They lived on the floor below, and whenever he wanted to ask Monique a question, her father, rather than picking up the phone, would bang on the floor and she would come running.

Monique and I were about the same age and became good friends. Her father tended to wave his hand imperiously over the details, but she missed nothing, so I came to depend on her careful mind. I learned about the items from Romaine's estate that they had inherited through her. There were some unfinished canvases, including one that was hardly more than a caricature, of the Marchesa Casati, whom everyone had painted. There was a delicate study of a nude, *The Weeping Venus,* named for a poem by Natalie Barney on the theme that nature makes martyrs out of women by condemning them to childbirth, a fate from which only death can release them. There were dozens of beautiful line drawings, undulating arabesques that Romaine had signed with her characteristic signature, a wing in flight. There was a treasure trove of photographs. There were forty-one trunks in all, full of clothes: fifty to sixty hats; sixty-two identical berets in different colors; ten or twelve pairs of new shoes; Moroccan and Chinese costumes; a dozen lounging pajamas in the same style in green, red, yellow and cream; and gloves, scarves, and other accessories. There were notebooks full of her pithy and mordant conclusions about mankind. There were about a hundred pounds of old pharmaceutical drugs; Romaine was an avid self-medicator. There were hundreds of letters, including Natalie's to her, and some souvenirs of Gabriele d'Annunzio, but none of his letters. Maître Léon-Marie Emanuel was willing to let me read everything, but insisted on supervising. The first day I sat on one side of an immaculately polished, empty table. Maître Emanuel sat opposite. One by one, he slid the documents, a page at a time, across the vast, shining space. Then he watched me taking notes. Pretty soon he was chatting away. Then he was laughing. After about an hour he stood up, bowed politely and went away. I was on my own.

I ended up making a great friend of Maître Emanuel as well. Beneath his formal manner was a lively intelligence, an irreverent wit and a certain impatience with correct behavior. I recall his laughing description of his mother-in-law's fondness for money with a hand gesture, thumb and forefinger rubbed together meaningfully, and his slang term, *de la galette,* which roughly translates as "filthy lucre" and went into our family lexicon. I joked that if I had been a bit older, or he a bit younger, I would have proposed, but I did not mean it; he was too autocratic for my taste. Still, he was a kind and tolerant parent and, for his generation, enlightened. He looked on "Tante Romaine" with much more understanding than her sister Maya had done. His mother-in-law was scandalized by Romaine's unorthodox love life, and their joint hatred of their mother was all they had in common. "Maya was as much a lady as Romaine was an artist," Philippe Grossin said. "She died with nine or ten servants in an enormous house, with fifty-eight rooms for herself." His wife added that Maya would summon her grandchildren for a visit and then expect to be entertained by them, whereas, when they visited Tante Romaine, she was the one who did the entertaining. "Maya was a very unhappy person, tied down by convention, locked in a prison, full of prejudices and prejudgments. She never tried to understand the forces that had molded her." For her part, Romaine kept an uneasy distance and did not reconcile with her niece Béatrice's family until Béatrice had died. Philippe Grossin was dispatched to convey the news of her death and deliver a letter by hand. For some reason there were no servants around. He banged on the door. With a great clanking of chains, the door opened a crack. A hand appeared, took the letter and shut the door. Asked how Romaine was, he replied, "She has a very young hand."

Maître Emanuel had read Romaine's letters with a certain amount of skepticism; while conceding that her mother had probably been an inadequate parent, he suspected that Romaine had exaggerated her ill treatment. What upset him was her claim to have lived in poverty. At one time, she wrote, she almost starved while waiting for the next check to arrive. This offended him because it cast aspersions on the family's good name. He insisted that she had received the same allowance as her sister, and that Maya had lived very comfortably. Tante Romaine's unorthodox love affairs were never really discussed, but it seemed from our conversations that they took a worldly-wise view. I was wrong about that. After the book was published I had a reproachful letter from Monique voicing the family's dismay that I had been so frank about this aspect of Tante Romaine's life. It was an early lesson in the equivocal position in which any biographer is placed; in order to borrow material, one needed to ingratiate oneself with people who were quite likely to detest one's work, an advance warning of what would happen in the case of Kenneth Clark. As for Maître Emanuel, I never heard from him after that.

I was always returning from trips with caches of information that I was dying to tell somebody, and my friends Matthew and Judy Huxley could be depended on to invite me for dinner and listen tolerantly. There is a picture of Matthew in the spring of 1928, taken just before he went off to school, being regarded by his immensely lanky and bespectacled father Aldous. Matthew, from his small, defiant height, arms folded, stares right back. That was Matthew when I knew him, ready to take on the world, a pose buried, more often than not, beneath a large, friendly guffaw. Judy, his second wife, bore a curious resemblance to Matthew's mother Maria, as I saw from the photographs in Sybille Bedford's biography of his father. When I first met Matthew and Judy, they were living in a kind of overgrown Chevy Chase bungalow surrounded by a large, unkempt garden, which, being passionate gardeners, they were strong-arming into submission inch by inch.

Their idiosyncratic house bore the same evolving imprint of their forceful personalities. The stairwell immediately did double duty as a library, and the living room was artfully arranged to accommodate a capacious dining area—they loved giving dinner parties. The next stage in their conviviality was to claim a porch as an impromptu dining room. That was fun but a bit cramped, so they reconfigured the house again, adding a very large dining room with French doors opening onto the back garden and a sort of porthole that was Matthew's folly. This addition ushered in a new and grander era in the Huxley literary salon: writers, photographers, Russian poets, the odd scientist or two—Matthew was an epidemiologist—and, latterly, diplomats. Judy gave a book party for my biography of Romaine, and managed to snag the Italian ambassador. One winter the British ambassador and his wife came to dinner and brought an English Christmas cake with a frilly red wrapper.

Matthew and Judith Huxley, 1965

Matthew had written a book with the photographer Cornell Capa about the jungle families on the Peruvian-Brazilian border, *Farewell to Eden.* It was well received, and after that Matt and I were always talking about writing a book together. One bibulous evening we had definitely decided on our subject, when Judy took me quietly aside. She said, "You know Matthew doesn't mean everything he says. Wait and see if he wants to do it tomorrow," and of course he didn't. So we never did write our book, but he did the next best thing. On one of our dinners I told him I had found an exercise book in which Romaine had written, "My dead mother gets between me and life. I speak as she desires, / I act as she commands / To me she is the root enemy of all things." I realized she had written this fifty years after her mother died. Matthew said, "There's the title of your book." "What?" I said. *"Between Me and Life."* And so it was.

The only photograph in Romaine's apartment when she died was of a handsome young man, signed "Roland." Monique

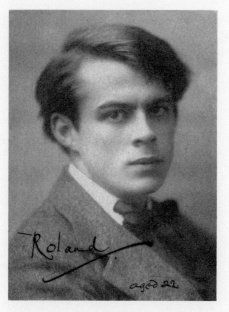

"Roland"

Grossin and I were intrigued, wondering what hold this man could have had on Romaine's imagination to be so prominently in her thoughts decades later. Monique thought it must be a photograph of her brother, St. Mar. I was sure it was not, but there seemed to be no clues to his identity in Romaine's admittedly disguised memoirs.

At about the same time I learned from Sir Harold Acton in Florence that one of the first portraits Romaine had ever painted was of John Fothergill, one of her few male friends. The portrait was "more virile than most," he said. He did not know where it was or whether it still existed. Sir Harold said, "Romaine told me that Fothergill came one day when she was out and stole the portrait." We both knew that Romaine never wanted to part with any of her work. I was immediately on the alert. If, as seemed likely, this was her first full-scale exploration of personality, then the painting would be a vital clue to her development as an artist. I decided I was going to find it.

Gifted in art and literature, John Fothergill was a protégé of

Oscar Wilde's, knew Lord Alfred Douglas, and spent a decade working for E. P. Warren, a wealthy American collector, helping him form an important collection of classical antiquities that is now at the Boston Museum of Fine Arts. Fothergill went on to become a collector in his own right, but of people. He established an inn at Thame, near Oxford, that became popular with dons and undergraduates, and a weekend retreat for artists, writers and politicians, and wrote three books about it. One of Fothergill's letters in later years to Romaine makes a reference to the fact that he still has her portrait, "to his shame," rather confirming Sir Harold's suspicions. Fothergill died in 1957, and finding his heirs was amazingly difficult. Although I knew he had two sons, I could not discover their whereabouts. It took months, but my persistence was finally rewarded when I tracked down one of them, Anthony Fothergill. At first he was puzzled. He did not remember seeing the portrait. A great many artists had painted his father. He would have to look through his father's effects. But a few days later he wrote to say they did indeed have the portrait. It was hanging in their living room. It was signed "Beatrice," Romaine's first name, and "Goddard," her maiden name. Her married name, Romaine Brooks, was on the back of the canvas. He would be happy to let me see it.

I bought a cheap second-class day return from London to Leicester, and Anthony Fothergill met me at the platform. I wrote, "Tony is a smile and a lot of gray hair and sideburns. His voice is slow, a bit woolly, foggy, indecisive, romantically vague, but behind it is a quick intelligence. He was wearing a big, comfortable turtleneck sweater and looked the image of the scientist who is puzzling the meaning of existence and has forgotten to tie his shoelaces."

He and his wife and children lived in a fourteenth- or fifteenth-century cottage of mellow rose brick, crazy support beams bent and twisted with age, and an impeccable garden behind it. There were very low ceilings—some of the beams were only five and a half feet from the floor—chintz slipcovers, a

The lost painting of John Fothergill
by Romaine Brooks, 1905

grandfather clock, handsome antique furniture, and hyacinths on the windowsill, laying down their heavy, glorious scent. His wife was quick, pretty, chirpy, efficient and bustling. She served a wholesome lunch of brown bread, farm-made local Leicester cheese and omelettes. There were two honey-colored female Pekingeses wagging their tails like flags, a black Persian cat and a guinea pig named Henry, with *-etta* added after she had babies.

After lunch we inspected the portrait. It was a formal study in the late-nineteenth-century academic tradition, and the only quality it had in common with Romaine's later work was its somber color scheme. The face was cameo-sharp against a black background, and the outlines of the shoulder and a bow at the neck were almost lost in the inky darkness. Nevertheless, the portrait was painted with confidence and a sure dramatic sense. Romaine caught, in the way the expression in the eyes contradicted the set of the mouth, a certain ambivalence, as if she sensed an inner bewilderment masked by the show of determination. There was the feeling of a perceptive imagination at work that I had not expected to find in this first major portrait.

It had not occurred to me that "Roland" and John Fothergill were one and the same until I learned that Fothergill's middle name was "Rowland." It had not occurred to Anthony Fothergill, either, to mention that they had a copy of his father's memoir, *Lest an Old Man Forget*. But his wife had thought of that. It was an easy matter to find the reference to a beautiful American girl he'd met in Rome called "B," and, once the clues were in place, to find a parallel account in *No Pleasant Memories* of a handsome English boy she'd met in Rome, "Ronald," supposedly. The discovery was worth all the effort. The two accounts tallied in remarkable ways. Romaine might have exaggerated her childhood, but at least in this case she appeared to have described events just as they happened. And it turned out that they had fallen in love. They were inseparable for months, and the Fothergills suspected they'd lived together. So did I. I had gone looking for a portrait and ended up connecting not only two disparate pieces of evidence, but documenting a relationship from both points of view, a feat I was seldom to duplicate. As for the reason why this should be the one photograph she wanted to look at seventy years later: some riddles, I found, will never be solved.

My base for these investigations was London. I was lucky enough to share a house with Barbara Mostyn, a friend of the

Huxleys, an American teaching and doing research in London. She was living in the garden of High Point, an apartment building designed by Lubetkin and Tecton, a prominent architectural firm of the 1930s that had also built such disparate projects as the penguin and polar bear houses at the London Zoo. High Point, appropriately named at the top of a hill, was characteristic of their free-flowing style and had become an Art Deco landmark. Bobbi's house was down below it, very Arizona in feeling, with its fifties-style picture windows, its bedrooms running off a balconied living room, equally incongruous when compared with its discreet eighteenth-century surroundings.

My stay in Highgate incidentally showed me the extent to which I was in danger of being submerged in my single-minded effort to uncover every detail of Romaine Brooks's life. Ron Hall, my editor friend at the *Sunday Times,* and I both liked to pub-crawl, and he had helped me feel almost at home in El Vino's in the days when women were stared at if they dared to stand at the bar and were relegated to tables in the back. One night he drove me to a party in an area of London I did not know and to which I had paid very little attention. It was a motley affair; liquor was flowing pretty freely and there was not much to eat. The next time I thought of looking, Ron was nowhere to be found. I discovered him curled up on a sofa staring besottedly at a very pretty girl beside him. Since he had brought me, I thought that was a bit much, and anyway it was past midnight. So I found my coat and left. But once I got onto the pavement, my head cleared marginally and I realized I had no idea where I was. I had a "London A-to-Z" map, but it was too dark to read it, and there seemed to be no street sign. Not a soul in sight.

Then I saw a car. I had grown up reading Enid Blyton's children's books and the continuing adventures of Noddy in Toyland. One drawing I remember was of a small, fat police car, traveling about three feet off the ground (to show you how fast it was going), with policemen in helmets brandishing truncheons from every window. In my befuddled state it looked like a drawing come to life; here was the same comical little car full of policemen, the only difference being that they weren't hanging out of windows. So I flagged them down. "Where am I?" I asked. "Where do you want to go?" they replied.

So I hopped in, sandwiched in the back seat between two muscular and rather attractive policemen, and described my destination. The driver made a U-turn and we set off. It was quite a long trip and I kept up a running monologue about what I was doing, what a wonderful story it was, how I was going to write this brilliant book, and other comments I squirm to recall. They finally pulled up beside my door and I staggered out. What they made of it all I don't dare to think.

I was always going somewhere, and after I reached Paris my destination became Gardone Rivera on the Lago di Garda. Among the souvenirs that Romaine's family found in her effects was a small, beautifully carved wooden box. It was locked and there seemed no way to open it, but then a tiny gold bar was also unearthed that, it was discovered, had been ingeniously designed to hide a key. Inside the box was an article about Romaine Brooks by D'Annunzio, written in his own hand. I knew that Romaine had painted two portraits of the Italian poet; this proof of just how precious his memory was presented another clue. What role had D'Annunzio played in her life? I had to find out.

Gabriele d'Annunzio, part artist, part man of action, is the kind of hero with which Italian history is replete and so unlikely anywhere else. He began life (as did Mussolini) as a journalist, showing an early talent for poetry, and published his first collection of poems, *Primo Vere,* at the age of sixteen. This was followed by more books of poetry, a trilogy of novels and then a

Romaine Brooks with Gabriele d'Annunzio, c. 1915

series of extremely popular plays. He had a passionate affair with Eleanora Duse, for whom he wrote several dramas, including *La Gioconda* and *La Città Morta*. By then he had been elected to parliament and during World War I became a pioneer in the art of aerial warfare; he was wounded several times and lost an eye. After the war, indignant that Italy had not been given Fiume, an Adriatic port on the border between Italy and Yugoslavia, D'Annunzio marched on the city and held it for fifteen months. He was an early supporter of Mussolini, who reciprocated by allowing D'Annunzio to spend his declining years beside the Lago di Garda building an estate, Il Vittoriale degli Italiani, which he subsequently gave to the nation.

By the time Romaine met him in 1908, D'Annunzio, ten years her senior, had a notorious reputation as a womanizer, known for his debts and extravagant lifestyle. Women found the combination of a man of action who could also bend his talents as a poet to seducing them, irresistible, which goes to show how little appearance counts for anything. His was distinctly unappetizing. He was short and somewhat plump, with narrow shoulders, rounded hips, pockmarked skin, and not much hair. Romaine met him at a lunch party given by an Italian poster artist, and would have ignored him completely, but then he said, of their host's gaudy palette, "And to think how much can be expressed without any color at all!" This naturally got her attention. She invited him to her studio and he began composing verses to each of her paintings in turn, praising their subtlety and insight into character. It was the beginning of a friendship that would last for thirty years.

There were 123 letters from Romaine Brooks to D'Annunzio at Il Vittoriale, and 148 telegrams. This naturally sharpened my curiosity since, apart from the article and one or two poems and photographs, none of D'Annunzio's letters to her had been found despite a thorough search. Or so Maître Emanuel said, and I believed him. But this was baffling, since Romaine kept almost everyone else's. Why would she have destroyed D'Annunzio's? This was naturally what Dr. Emilio Mariano, keeper of the flame at Il Vittoriale, wanted to know, and there was no satisfactory answer. Mariano was conducting a negotiation of such delicacy that it took me a while to see what was happening. He was sure that Maître Léon-Marie was, as the expression goes, holding out on him. I must be, in some way, an emissary of Romaine's heirs. Perhaps he thought they intended to sell the letters they professed not to have—and assuming that they had found roughly the same number, these would have fetched a pretty penny on the market—and so the plan was to tantalize me. I could read but not copy, look but not touch. After I had put the predictable pressure on the French family and after Mariano got the letters he wanted, I would get what I wanted. It was never stated this way. All the letters were extravagantly polite. Nevertheless, this was the hidden message. I was the pawn.

None of this dawned on me at the time. All I knew was that

I would be allowed to read Romaine's letters. So I set off hopefully for Italy, taking the train as far as Milan, and then renting a car. I drove to Il Vittoriale one evening in late fall through a blizzard. The countryside out of Milan is a monotonous plain broken by an occasional crumbling farm building or church tower. The cold had stripped the earth bare, and clouds rolled down and smothered it; snow fogged the landscape like smoke, and I drove into a void.

I awoke next morning in Gardone to a clear blue sky. I looked out of my hotel window onto flowers, olive trees in fruit, palms, the orange-tiled roofs of buildings and walls bleeding orange and brown; a lake glittered in the still air. The foothills of the Alps were in the background, covered with snow, but through some fluke of nature the area surrounding the lake has a subtropical climate and leaves stay on the trees all year. The perimeter of the lake has been developed with expensive hotels, but a kilometer up the hillside is the old village of Gardone, looking for all the world like Act I Scene I of *The Barber of Seville.* Here are the narrow, winding streets, wrought-iron balconies, ruined walls gently crumbling under the weight of a lushly flowering rose, the creaking lanterns and rotund peasants in soiled blue overalls and caps seated at tables outside a trattoria. It hardly seemed real. And across from this village, rising against a tapestry of Lombardy poplars and blue-green hills, was D'Annunzio's estate, the Victory Monument of the Italians.

I spent several days there and, once I had entered the gates of this preposterous poet's playground, it took that long for me to recover from my stupefaction. Il Vittoriale is a fantastic memorial to one man's megalomania, a sinister ship of death. Inside it D'Annunzio sealed every random act of his life, barricading himself against the horror of oblivion. Here are arches, columns, walls, allegorical statuary, pillars, tombs, fountains, steps, bells, tiled courtyards and paths. Here is a museum, a library, an amphitheatre for his plays, and a mausoleum, looking like a half-submerged submarine, for his mortal remains and those of ten others who fought with him in World War I. A pillar commemorates a rearguard battle he fought at Piave. A plane in which he flew over Vienna on a propaganda raid hangs in the auditorium. The Fiat in which he guided his followers into battle is mounted in the courtyard. Even the boat that figured in the assault on Fiume was disassembled, plank by plank, and rebuilt on the hillside overlooking the lake.

But it was his villa, situated in an old country house, in which his passion for demonic excess made itself felt most acutely. Cecil Beaton, who photographed it, complained in his diaries that he came away exhausted; "the airlessness, the slightly dusty veneer and the mothballs," combined with an atmosphere that was macabre and almost evil, produced an actual pain in his chest. It was easy to see why. Each room had been attacked in garish colors with suffocating draperies and over-ornamented geometrical motifs, festooned with scraps of poetry and homilies running under the picture rails, and furnished with Chinese figurines, bejeweled Florentine plaster casts, moth-eaten animal skins and gold lamé. Yet as Beaton also saw, the house was jammed with books, thirty thousand of them, many annotated and a testament to D'Annunzio's intellectual life. There was no escaping his presence. His private quarters still preserved the moment of his death in 1938, more than half a century ago. Here sat the spectacles on the writing desk, the quill pens, the pencils, the toothbrushes and soap. The Chinese silk robes he liked to wear, carefully pressed and mothballed, hung in the wardrobe. Each object on his bedside table was placed exactly as he had left it. The last written papers and the last works in preparation were laid out carefully on his studio table. There were ancient retainers who turned on lights and unlocked doors to show visitors inside, then turned off lights and locked the doors carefully as one left. In the end one could hardly breathe.

The shock of Il Vittoriale was enough, but then I discovered something that made everything else fade from my mind. As I read Romaine's letters (in French, the language they used), I realized I was reading the story of a love affair. Their friendship had begun in an entirely undemanding way. They had simply enjoyed being with each other, discussing poetry, literature, the theatre and art. She wrote, "Like you, I don't laugh any more. Do you remember how we used to spend hours laughing with each other? How delightful you were! I remember each change of mood on your face, so full of charm and infinite expression." But by degrees her pleasure in his company became an overwhelming passion. She wrote about how much she loved him, and that she wanted to cover his naked body with fruit. She was insanely in love, and in a letter that was almost incoherent, she concluded, "I'll succeed in getting you or I'll die." Even though unsigned, the handwriting was unmistakable. Having learned how much Romaine Brooks shrank from intimate male contact (she wrote, "The sexual act is a commotion, rather than an emotion"), it seemed unbelievable. I had to have those letters. Dr. Mariano did not waver. I should identify the ones I wanted to have photocopied. I would have to wait and see. There was nothing more I could do.

The love affair ended for the predictable reason: like any other Don Juan, D'Annunzio was easily bored. Romaine saw the pattern emerge and managed to extricate herself. (She did it by seducing Ida Rubinstein, another of the ladies he wanted, and it gave her vast satisfaction.) I wish I could have dismissed D'Annunzio that easily, but I could not get Romaine's letters to him out of my mind. On the other hand, Maître Emanuel was sure there were no letters from him to her, and that seemed to doom my hopes. I wrote letters to everyone I could think of. I was eventually introduced to Gil Tatge, the wife of an American diplomat stationed in Milan, who said she would help, and did. She went to Il Vittoriale and convinced Dr. Mariano that Romaine must have destroyed D'Annunzio's letters, as we all concluded. To this day I do not know how she did it, but she prevailed. I got copies of the letters, about one-third of the total. Dr. Mariano got nothing from Maître Emanuel. The chapter was saved.

It took me two years and several false starts to hammer out the right style for the biography. In time I would come to enjoy the challenge, not to mention the luxury of a leisurely introduction and those touches of detail that are usually cut from newspaper and magazine articles. I wanted to give some kind of outline of this personality, based on so many disparate impressions. Bettina Bergery's comment that Romaine's eyes were like pistol shots, like Picasso's, had to be balanced against a photograph I had acquired of Romaine on Capri in 1900, garlanded with laurels, wearing a white robe, smiling shyly, her eyes wide and soft. There was another portrait of her in 1908 as a lady of fashion, wearing a feather-trimmed Gibson Girl hat and an ermine-trimmed robe, jeweled and braceleted. There was yet another photograph, in the 1920s, posed against a wall, one leg casually slung over it, in a handsome striped robe, elegant and not quite mannish.

I thought of her comment, *"Je suis sur la table ou sous la table, ne disant rien."* I recalled the taped interview I had been given of her voice, still amused and vital, singing and cracking jokes, at the age of ninety-three. I thought of the poem D'Annunzio wrote for her, which included the lines *"Nul sort ne domptera, ni par fer ni par flamme, / le secret diamant de ton coeur ingénu."* I thought of the visit I had made to Somerset Maugham's companion, Alan Searle, when he was ill in a Monte Carlo hospital. He was the one who joked that when Romaine kissed you she put her tongue down your throat, which did not appear to upset him in the slightest. He had wanted to marry her. He turned in his bed to find her letters, exposing a substantial area of pink

The dining room at 20, rue Jacob showing the garden beyond, with a drawing of Natalie Barney propped against the window

bottom. I thought of Sir Compton MacKenzie, whom I had gone to visit in Edinburgh, and who had made Romaine the heroine of one of his novels set in Capri, *Extraordinary Women*. We talked one long afternoon about Maugham and Munthe and all the personalities of those far-off days. Sir Compton was blind by then, but still a dogged conversationalist who, if obliged to listen, would indicate his impatience by twirling a red handkerchief with increasing violence. He was the one who made me aware that "extraordinary" in this sense was the adjective one used out of politeness, when what one really meant was "bizarre beyond belief."

I happened to think Romaine really was extraordinary. Somehow I would have to find the right compositional structure if I was going to give a faithful portrait of this personality with all her strengths and weaknesses, her charm and stubborn complexity, and the grandeur and pathos of her life. Most of all, I needed letters and these, as I was to learn, are always a problem. Even though copyright laws protect unpublished writings, and the owners do not quite know what you can do with them, they are sure there must be something, so they hold on to them just in case. If the writers are still alive, one can hope for an interview as some sort of substitute, but sometimes, as in the case of Romaine and D'Annunzio, letters are the only remaining witnesses. I was naturally determined to get my hands on Romaine's letters to Natalie. Natalie at that point was past caring, but Janine Lahovary, her literary executor, had her own ideas. She definitely did not want me to see them.

Natalie Barney had lived on rue Jacob since 1909. The street was once called the Chemin du Pré aux Clercs and, later, rue du Colombier, and dates from the Middle Ages. Her house, at least three hundred years old, was hidden from the street by heavy wooden doors and at the far edge of a courtyard; it was popularly, but erroneously, believed to have been the home of the actress Adrienne Lecouvreur (1692–1730), a great interpreter of Racine.

What made Number 20 a kind of miracle on the Left Bank was its garden, an oasis in a jungle of winding streets, a remnant of the great seventeenth- and eighteenth-century gardens that once stretched from rue Jacob down to the Seine. "You can't believe the charm of the house," Bettina Bergery said. "First of all, there was a curtain of ivy over the walls and a huge tree in the courtyard, now chopped down, that hung over the house. There was this lovely rambling garden with its eighteenth-century temple, and it dominated the house. Inside, one found a green aquarian light. Everything was subdued and warm. Plus a big, greedy table of food where we all used to eat like mad."

It seemed to be transfixed, this house on rue Jacob, at the moment when the visitor stepped through the door off the street, crossed the cobbled courtyard and was greeted by

Madame Berthe, Natalie's factotum, who remembered everyone's name, and had wandered into the salon, vaguely red and packed with sofa beds covered in brown velvet, with lavish fur throws, tapestries, portraits, photographs and mirrors. Here was the grand piano on which Wanda Landowska and Darius Milhaud had played, and there was a bust of Natalie's close friend, the poet Milosz. On the wall was a portrait of Natalie as a page at the age of eleven, painted by Carolus Duran, her mother Alice Pike Barney's art teacher. Objects sank into a perpetual semi-darkness because, Natalie wrote, "I have lived in the twilight and when I am not there, my things are sleeping." Everything would be overcast with a faint air of disarray or neglect. At least three photograph albums belonging to Colette, and dating from 1905 to 1910, were heaped about on a coffee table; friends said they had been there for years. A lingering trace of someone's Oriental perfume mingled with the smell of roses wilting in a vase. There would be a box of chocolates, half-eaten, on a table beside a lute the strings of which were broken. I pulled out a volume of Natalie's aphorisms from a bookcase and out fell a bathing cap, a relic of the 1930s, the kind my mother wore.

Madame Berthe showed me around, torn between pride at the history of the house, its air of luxury and refined associations, and anger at the treatment she had received. When she became ill and needed an operation, Madame Lahovary used this as a pretext to move Natalie out of the house she had lived in for sixty years, into a suite at the Meurice. Madame Berthe trembled as she described what she found once she was well enough to go back into the house. The kitchen had been cleaned out and all her cooking utensils were gone, *"même mes Pyrex!"* she said in horror. As for the house, paintings were gone, including one of Romaine's that was prominently displayed on an easel. Chairs had vanished. Statues were removed. Where they went she did not know, but she had her suspicions, she said meaningfully. Behind the scenes she was my ally. Whatever Janine Lahovary did not want me to do was good enough. So she showed me where Romaine's letters were hidden; there were drawers and cupboards full of them all over the house. I smuggled them out a batch at a time until I had several hundred. By the time I received Natalie Barney's permission to read them, I had them all. As each group was rounded up, I headed straight for my small hotel room, sat on my bed and covered myself with them. I could not have felt any richer if I had just broken the bank at Monte Carlo.

As I made my trips back to the house, I was trying to reconstruct those Friday-afternoon receptions that Bettina Bergery had told me about, when there might be anything from twenty to a hundred people and they would somehow seat them all. Madame Berthe would make sumptuous chocolate cakes and harlequin-colored cupcakes and triangular sandwiches "folded up like damp handkerchiefs," Bettina Bergery said. There would be tea, whiskey and pitchers of fruit cup, and the Duchesse de Clermont-Tonnerre would preside at one end, pouring regal cups of tea, and the green half-light from the garden would filter into the room, reflecting off the glasses and the silver tea urn as from underwater. In my mind's eye I saw Cocteau, Proust, Paul Valéry and André Gide and all those others Romaine liked or disliked.

There would be Dolly Wilde, Oscar's niece, seated next to the old historian Professor Seignobos and drawing him out on the subject of *Lady Chatterley's Lover,* the only novel he had ever read. I thought of Renée Vivien, the young poet Natalie loved, who died so tragically young, and Colette in old age, "wearing sandals, with toes like bunches of carrots," and droning on interminably about her mother, according to Bettina. Bit by bit the illusion grew that the house was full of presences. The party was over, but there were still snatches of departing conversations, of footsteps crossing back over the courtyard, of glasses clinking in the kitchen, and Natalie would be going upstairs to bed. That

room had a gray and white starred bedspread, matching the curtains on the French windows, and a pale oval ceiling; there was a
tiara askew on top of a wardrobe, a clutter of letters and a china
vase in the shape of a white swan. And somewhere on the circular staircase with its brown velvet rope, something came into
focus in my mind. I realized that the atmosphere of the house
had made me a part of it and given me the sharpest possible
image, perhaps transitory but unmistakably clear. I suddenly
saw what it was like to be living then.

Chapter Six

Truth Against the World

Somewhere in my files I have a photograph of myself at the reopening ceremonies for one of Frank Lloyd Wright's Usonian houses, his idiosyncratic solution to the problem of how to build cheaply. The Pope-Leighey residence, so called for its two owners, was in the path of a new Virginia highway, Route 66. So, to spare it from demolition, the National Park Service found a new location on the grounds of Woodlawn Plantation, and it was opened to the public in 1964. A great deal of trouble had been taken over a minor demonstration of the great man's art, which would have given him a laugh. Wright always scoffed at historic preservation, but then he was an architect.

I was seated in the audience wearing my new navy and white checked wool suit and a studious expression, one masking the fact that I had no idea what was going on. I certainly did not know enough to realize that the building had been wrongly aligned in terms of the compass, ruining the calculated play of light and shade through its clerestory windows, and, because the house was now on a downhill slope, presenting an ugly flat roof to the visitor that was never meant to be seen. What I did notice was the absurdly small kitchen area, hardly a room, and bedrooms minuscule even by ocean-liner, tourist-class standards.

Frank Lloyd Wright
in the prime of life, c. 1930

Still, there was something very delightful about the intricately angled living room and its carved woodwork even if the house was, as everyone said, ridiculously expensive for a mass-produced building. It seemed of a whole in its tiny perfection, obviously the work of an artist.

Years passed. I don't remember now how it happened, but in 1987 I got it into my head that Wright would be a wonderful subject for a biography. There were three good reasons why this seemed to be a terrible idea. The first was given by my former colleague at the *Washington Post,* Sarah Booth Conroy, who knew as much about the inner workings of Taliesin, Wright's foundation, as anybody at the paper. After Wright died in 1959, the informal group of architects and apprentices re-formed around Olgivanna Lloyd Wright, a Montenegran beauty, grand-daughter of a general, who had a whim of iron. Those who tangled with her left; those who stayed knew Mrs. Wright's crotchets and quirks to the letter and were unlikely to approve of any book that was indiscreet, and there were plenty of areas of Wright's messy life that she had successfully suppressed. So, even though Olgivanna Wright had died—in 1985—and the coast was presumably clear, Sarah Booth thought her influence was as strong as ever. I also learned that Wright's archive at the foundation was a treasure trove, but that anyone doing research there was charged one hundred dollars an hour, a serious disincentive. Finally, Brendan Gill, architecture critic at *The New Yorker,* an old family friend, was about to publish his own monument to Wright's memory, *Many Masks.* In publishing terms, that pretty well ruled out a new book. Or so I thought.

I discovered to my surprise that one of the first acts of the foundation under Richard Carney, its chief executive officer, William Wesley Peters, chairman of its board of trustees, and Bruce Brooks Pfeiffer, its archivist, had been to undercut Mrs. Wright in a discreet but stunning way. They had agreed to have Wright's archive transferred to the Getty Center Archives for the History of Art and the Humanities, then in Santa Monica. The agreement was that the Getty would put the archive on microfiche and then make it available to scholars; in other words, Taliesin was relinquishing control. In fact, that project had just been concluded when I thought up my bright idea in 1987, one of the few times when my timing has been impeccable. Dr. Nicholas Olsberg, director of the Getty Archives, was anxious to have someone come and study there. I could stay as long as I liked, he said. His invitation was pressing.

After I read Gill's *Many Masks,* more of an attenuated essay or disquisition than a biography as such, there were other reasons to think there was room for another book. It was clear that a warm personal relationship had existed between the author and

Olgivanna and
Frank Lloyd Wright, 1940s

Olgivanna Wright. The biographer was much less enthusiastic about his subject. While admiring his work, Gill thought this was someone who hid behind disguises, self-mythologizing, a teller of lies, restless, mischievous, manic, disruptive and an artful dodger. On the other hand, Olgivanna was disciplined, strong, benign and gallant, the high priestess of the shrine her husband had created. In time I would come to believe that *Many Masks* applied much more accurately to Olgivanna than to her husband. It was enough to know that a book had been written from her perspective. Gill presumably could have used the Wright archive, but had not. That left the field open to someone to write a biography from Wright's point of view.

American authors, by and large, had seen Wright as a product of New England Transcendentalist thought, coming as it did from his Unitarian minister father, William Carey Wright. This surprised me. In the first place, his father's influence on his life ended when he left Wright's mother and siblings. But, from childhood, Wright had been surrounded by the equally strong influences of his ten Welsh aunts and uncles—and his mother was born in Wales. Surely the Welsh, i.e., Celtic, sense of the dream of things, of another state of being, the animism of Celtic thought, the belief in the divine in every leaf and tree, was just as formative an influence. Coming from Bath, in the west of England, I knew about Welsh poetry, music, language and history. I knew the Welsh to be impulsive, brave, mercurial and full of imaginative fancy, valiant in defeat and self-destructive only when goaded beyond endurance. I knew the Welsh. Frank Lloyd Wright was a Welshman; I was sure of it.

Jennifer Josephy, my editor and friend for the past decade, wanted to do the book but was overruled by her publisher because of Gill's book. That was upsetting, but then Murray Pollinger showed my outline to Robert Gottlieb, who happened to be in London. The editor-in-chief at Knopf was about to leave, to become editor at *The New Yorker*. He paid no attention to what was in print, and in the end my book did not appear for five years, making for a perfectly respectable publishing interval. He handed me over to Victoria Wilson, daughter of an American author and stepdaughter of Stella Adler. Her many interests include a love of art and the theatre, and I would have a long and happy collaboration with her. Finally, Carmen Callil in London bought the book for Chatto & Windus. The omens could not have looked brighter.

Everyone knew that after their final defeat at the hands of the Normans in the thirteenth century, the Welsh had lived with their backs to the sea, despised and ridiculed by their conquerors. I did not know that the Lloyd Jones family were, in religious terms, a minority within a minority. They came from a small community in Wales that had been called the "black spot of Socinianism" because they followed the teaching of Fausto Sozzini (1539–1604) that there was no Holy Trinity but simply One God, and Christianity was just one of many paths toward enlightenment. Other Welsh Nonconformists—Calvinistic Methodists, Baptists and Congregationalists—considered them heretics as long as they were in Wales, a compelling reason to leave. Arriving in the New World, they were no better off, expelled from churches wherever they went. So they kept moving westward, finally settling in an idyllic valley not far from Spring Green, Wisconsin. It also explains their consuming ambition to build a church. They needed builders and architects long before Frank appeared on the scene. They wanted the right to worship freely. It was their Truth—Against the World.

Here was someone with whose beliefs I was in instinctive sympathy, but if the subject had its own mesmeric allure, the prospect was intimidating. I was no architectural historian. Wright's career began in adolescence and had not ended the day he died, at age ninety-one, with his culminating work, the Guggenheim Museum, still unfinished. I was more than willing to immerse myself, but was willingness enough? How was I to unravel the labyrinthine links between the life and the work, one of my central interests? One of the fascinating aspects of Symons's *Quest for Corvo* is the connection he draws between Rolfe's grandiose fantasies and the subject of his literary talents; in compensating for an ignominious reality, Rolfe incidentally created a work of art. The same could be said for Salvador Dalí, whose psychosexual struggles had made for some astonishing paintings; once he abandoned his themes, his work lost its hypnotic power. Every immigrant hounded from his native land wants to create a new and better home, a paradise to compensate for the hopes destroyed. Was this enough to explain a lifelong passion? "Organic architecture" was Ruskin's theme. By what alchemy had it become Wright's?

Kenneth Clark wrote that if he had to believe a minister of housing or the buildings put up in his time, he would believe the buildings. Taking this as my cue, I went to the Lloyd Jones valley

Unity Chapel

in Iowa County, outside Spring Green, to see two buildings. The first was Unity Chapel, the small church the family built on its former meeting grounds, and where most of them are now buried. Whether Wright's mother, Anna, actually hung lithographs of churches around his crib is a moot point, but it is certainly true that from childhood Wright was convinced of his future direction and, when he found that the family could finally afford to build a chapel, wanted to design it. His uncle, Jenkin Lloyd Jones, a Unitarian minister, was not about to let that happen, but Wright always claimed the ceilings, designed in squares, were his own invention. He was nineteen.

Uncle Jenk, who was already building in Chicago, hired his architect, J. Lyman Silsbee, to design Unity Chapel in a much-simplified version of the picturesque shingle style in which Silsbee specialized. The exterior shingles were a mottled brown and the roof was dark red. This must account for the fact that even though the chapel stands on open ground, when I went there it appeared to be in shadow. One entered a freestanding gate—if

there had been a fence, it was long gone—and along a path leading directly to the main entrance of the chapel, hardly dis-
cernible beneath the penumbral shade of a heavy porch. One
thought of the painting by René Magritte in which, despite a sky
of azure blue, buildings huddle in darkness on a deserted street;
there was such an air of stubborn desolation about a modest
building that symbolized so much passion, persistence and pain.
And everywhere there were graves, of Wright's grandparents,
who had brought the family across the sea; of his mother, aunts,
uncles, cousins, sisters (Maginel and Jane); and of most of his
children. As for his own grave, that was more prominent than
any of the others. I found a semicircle of flowers, neatly tended,
surrounding a planting of shrubbery and a single marking stone
bearing the words "Love of an idea is love of God." The grave
was empty.

"Oh yes, that damn business," said Elizabeth Wright Ingra-
ham, daughter of Wright's son John, herself an architect and
chairman of the family corporation established to oversee the
chapel. She was referring to the fact that in recent years, and to
escape the harsh Wisconsin winters, Wright had established a
second home, a camp outside Phoenix in the Arizona desert,
Taliesin West, as it was called. Olgivanna Lloyd Wright had
never liked Spring Green much, and after her husband's death
she had stayed in Taliesin West for longer and longer periods.
She would be cremated and buried there, and she wanted her
husband to join her.

This dying wish, in the nature of a dictate, contradicted
those of her husband, who had been designing his own memorial, which he was going to call Unity Temple, as his final resting
place on the Taliesin estate. He was making preliminary sketches
when he was in his eighties, but since he never wanted to think
about dying, there was no rush. The work poked along. An allée
of trees was planted, and it is said that one can still see the outline marking the spot on the ground where the temple was to

View of Taliesin from the lake, Spring Green, Wisconsin

stand. Oh, well. He had died a quarter of a century before, and Mrs. Wright had long since assumed command. Apprentices drove up to Spring Green with an exhumation order and had the master removed from his grave, cremated and driven back to the suburb of Scottsdale and Taliesin West. The family was up in arms. Newspapers wrote editorials; it was the equivalent of "uprooting Jefferson from Monticello for reburial in Beverly Hills," one wrote. The state of Wisconsin asked for the return of the remains. Carney and Peters were astonished at all the fuss. To Carney in Taliesin West, it was simple: "If Mrs. Wright said that is the burying ground, we have to come here." Never mind that Wright had written of the valley, "I still feel myself as much a part of it as the trees and birds." It was perhaps not surprising that, twenty-five years after his death, the architect who was embroiled in controversy all his life should be in the center of another partisan split.

The second building I wanted to see was Taliesin East, the house on the side of a hill that Wright began building in 1911 on the left bank of the Wisconsin River, and that survived fire after fire to rise again, rebuilt in ever-increasing complexity, with its broad sweeps of windows, interlocking terraces and jutting balconies. The word *Taliesin* can be translated as "shining brow," and in later years Wright would explain that it expressed his belief one should build in harmony with nature, on the side of a hill, rather than on top of it. But the word is also the name of a sixth-century Welsh bard of mythical status, a kind of poet-hero, although that aspect of the Wright equation, the Welsh identification, is usually ignored. It is certainly possible to perceive in the siting of his famous home, now a vast, gently decaying complex of buildings, a Celtic reverence for the sacredness of place. One approached the building from below by flights of stone steps, worn and covered with lichen; low doors tucked inconspicuously into the sides of thick stone façades reinforced the impression that one had stumbled on an ancient castle. This feeling intensified as one discovered that this seldom-used building was inhabited by thousands of swifts. They shot across one's path, soared up into the branches and spiraled around the massive chimneys with a curious chittering sound. And although Taliesin had been rebuilt so many times, when I went there in 1987 it was sliding into decay. The stones making up the foundation were tilting. The plaster was crumbling. The floors had shifted. The stonework was obscured by decades of dirt and lichen. Mold was eating away at the old beams. Windows no longer fitted their frames. Latches were sprung, toilets did not flush, and everywhere the birds were nesting in the chimneys.

Taliesin might be "supremely natural," as its creator claimed, but it was artful. Walking through the private quarters of the architect and his family made one realize that to fully appreciate his wizardry, one had to experience it. One then saw the way the low entrance hall gave one a glimpse of bright spaces beyond, the way the living room ceiling soared upward, the panoramic views over the valley and the way interior spaces were cleverly divided into nooks and crannies that tempted one to curl up with a book or engage in quiet conversation. And, for all its intricacy, the suite of rooms had an overall coherence. There were the same uses of stone, plaster, stucco, dark wooden beams, low benches, built-in shelves, cabinets, Oriental carpets, gold-leafed wall coverings, Japanese screens, Oriental pottery and objets d'art; the same soft tans, bronzes, leaf greens and omnipresent Taliesin reds. There was the same sense of acute stillness in the house, as if the owners had only just left and were about to return, a breathing silence. "Again, Taliesin!" he wrote. "Three times built, twice destroyed, yet a place of great repose. . . . I get back to it happy to be there again."

If Taliesin in Spring Green stood for a sense of belonging and clan loyalties, then Wright's home and studio in Oak Park, outside Chicago, represented his first successful forays into architecture as Louis Sullivan's apprentice and the establishment of his own household. There one sees evidence of the restless creativity that was to build, tear down, remodel, evolve and transform itself in a dozen different directions during a long career, along with the gradual development of steadfast underlying principles. I began to see that he was in the forefront of American architects who were, like their British counterparts, reacting against the ugliness and meaningless clutter of cheap mass production at the end of the nineteenth century. An overall concept, a single unifying theme, became his watchword, also that of the Arts and Crafts movement, as outlined in the writings of William Morris and John Ruskin. Organic architecture, truth to materials, enclosing and protective roofs, the central importance of the fireplace—these would become Wright's realities in his first Prairie houses.

His focus was always on the house as home, an outgrowth of his vision of the perfect marriage, surrounded by beauty in a hidden paradise. There was a certain circular logic to his reasoning. A perfect couple would naturally choose to live in a perfectly beautiful house. On the other hand, the perfect house would necessarily inspire and foster a perfect marriage. Expecting this much of a concept, however ideally realized, seems irrational nowadays, but it contained a hidden obsession. A great deal of Wright's hopes and expectations were bound up with his mother's failed relationship. He would build anew, create a more perfect existence to compensate them both for so much past unhappiness.

Wright's mother, Anna, is usually painted as a wholly positive force in his life, and it is true that she nurtured and encouraged him, believing in his gifts from the very beginning. In her eyes he could do no wrong, and this had its hidden costs. At the same time he had a moral obligation to live up to her exalted image of him, impossibly idealistic and certainly out of the reach of mere mortals. He must want what she wanted, love the things she loved and hate the people she hated, including his own father. That his father disappeared from his life has to be put down to Anna's destructive influence. She was living out her own failed hopes in her son, which made him a kind of captive and an uneasy mediator between her needs and his wife's rightful claims. As more and more children arrived, young Catherine, who had seemed the ideal girl, became any ordinary mother struggling with a husband who remodels the house every Tuesday, a manipulative and disapproving mother-in-law and six children all competing for her attention. By 1904 the marriage is in trouble, as one can see from a photograph of the family group; Catherine is surrounded by their brood, and the great man, wearing a smock and flowing tie, sits at a small but distinct distance. Another woman has come between them. She is Mamah Borthwick Cheney, a neighbor, married, with two children, and Wright had built the Cheneys a house.

Having rejected the boringly chronological approach to

biography, I had not appreciated the fact that there really are pivotal moments in a person's life when a single decision alters the future irrevocably. For Wright the date was 1909, when he left his wife and children and ran off with Mamah Borthwick Cheney. Just a year before, he was, according to a neighbor, considered a model citizen in Oak Park, "clean-hearted, clean-minded and with high ideals." By 1912 this wife-deserter was almost a criminal, shunned by all right-thinking people. His architectural practice was in a shambles and his direction as an artist was about to change radically. He was just forty-two.

One has to wonder how safe it was to know Wright too well, whether as a spouse, mistress, apprentice or devoted friend. Catherine was left penniless, with a grocery bill of nine hundred dollars, to struggle along as best she could—Frank's ability to hold on to money being as capricious as his affections. Mamah Cheney, who threw in her lot uncomplainingly with his, would end up brutally murdered, along with her two children, in 1914—another pivotal date. Close friends would be bankrupted, battle lawsuits or be afflicted with terrible accidents; such were the consequences of being pulled into the orbit of this powerful, profligate and charismatic personality. Perhaps they could not help themselves, swept into the whirlwind surrounding some-one they must have thought more like a force of nature. Well, genius does what it must, as the poet Edward Bulwer-Lytton liked to say. They must have known that this reckless giant was at his magnificent best when most at risk, too often up to his neck in water of his own boiling. He triumphed in the end, but it was a near thing. He had, he once wrote to his mother, a sense of foreboding and a waking dream "wherein we all seem som-nambulists, walking innocently on the ridges of churches and the edges of precipitous banks."

One can occasionally say that the next best thing to knowing someone personally is reading their letters. Most letter writers, of course, say very little, and a good argument can be made that the world's most boring book is *The Collected Letters of Bernard Berenson.* On the other hand, for everything B.B. did not say—he wrote reams, carefully sifted through that calculating mind so as to reveal nothing of value—his wife Mary provided the necessary insights, with her chatty, revealing and sometimes malicious accounts to their many friends and family members. A biographer always hopes for clues to inner states of mind, and in Wright's case they were there in the Taliesin Archive, particularly in the letters to Anna. It was as if Wright needed pen and paper to find out what he was really thinking, and everything poured out: his hopes, dreams, fears, boasts, brickbats and lively humor. The tone is so idiosyncratic and singular that, paradoxically, it became predictable. One of the *bons mots* ascribed to Wright's principal secretary, Eugene Masselink, was that he could write as good a Wright letter as Wright himself. Be that as it may, the existence of this lively, opinionated and self-revelatory archive led me far closer to the inner Wright than I had ever expected to get. And often his most anguished thoughts went to his mother. "I have had a terrible quest for the repose of heart and mind that meant *home* to me," he wrote. "Have waded through rivers of tears and blood to find it with a ruthlessness seldom if ever heard of—but always with a fool's sincerity and hope at least and a man's courage."

When he wrote about rivers of blood, Wright meant it literally. Seven years before the letter was written, in August 1914, a demented servant at Taliesin who was being dismissed, serving lunch as his last act, murdered Mamah Borthwick Cheney, her children John and Martha, and four employees: a foreman, a draftsman, a carpenter and a gardener. Then he set Taliesin ablaze. The famous tragedy became the subject of so many accounts, a documentary and even an opera, that the likelihood of uncovering anything new was remote. But fortunately there was still an eyewitness at one remove, Herbert Fritz, a Taliesin architect whose father had been there. And in those days before the newsreel, newspapers gave such stories the kind of blow-by-blow account that is only accorded to horse races nowadays. So in the frenzy of big-city and national attention, researchers appeared to have overlooked the small weekly papers closest to the actual events. In addition to the *Home News* of Spring Green, there were the *Weekly News* in nearby Baraboo and the *Dodgeville Chronicle,* not to mention the *Wisconsin State Journal* in Madison. Not many copies of these ancient newspapers could be found anywhere except on the remote shelves of the home offices (probably thrown out now, since the advent of the computer), but they repaid the search, being full of additional details. They were particularly useful in sketching out the background of the murderer, Julian Carlton, and providing some sort of motive for his crazed behavior. As for the rivers of tears to which Wright referred, I could find no clue to his state of mind—he was in Chicago that day and seems not to have been interviewed afterwards. All I knew was that he stoically went to one funeral after another. Then I discovered something important in the *Dodgeville Chronicle,* dated two weeks after the event. It made me realize not only how suicidal Wright had become, but also that he had still wanted to live.

Two of the quips repeated most often about Wright's houses came from Richard Lloyd Jones, a cousin who was founder of the *Tulsa Tribune,* and Jones's wife, whose name happened to be George. Since the rainfall in Tulsa was low, Wright apparently felt it was perfectly safe to give his creation, Westhope, a flat roof. Still, it does rain there sometimes, and flat roofs notoriously leak. The story went that in the middle of a downpour, Richard Lloyd Jones called up his cousin in a rage. "Frank," he said, "it's raining on my desk." "Move your desk," was the reply. In the middle of another rainstorm, George is said to have moved through the house positioning bowls and pans to catch the drips. "Oh well," she said, "this is what we get for leaving a work of art out in the rain." The quip eventually reached the architect's ears, and, being Wright, he filed it away for future reference. That moment came after he had visited the famous all-glass house in New Canaan, Connecticut, designed by Philip Johnson, an adherent of the International Style. Wright was no admirer of that style or of Johnson particularly, either; Johnson had once called him the greatest architect of the *nineteenth* century, well into the twentieth. "Ah yes, Philip," Wright said. "You're the man who builds those little houses and leaves them out in the rain."

Wright is frequently praised for having popularized the open plan, that concept now universal in which walls of any description have given way to vast interior spaces, usually accompanied by cathedral ceilings. But these interiors, in the context of noisemakers that hardly existed when Wright began designing—dishwashers, washing machines, vacuum cleaners, radios, telephones, stereo systems and the like—put everyone in the house at the mercy of the person making the noise. And not every parent enjoys being in the middle of constant chaos. The first house built for Herbert Jacobs, a history professor at the University of Wisconsin, considered the first "Usonian" house, is full of such stylistic advances. But for Jacobs's family of five children there was no privacy. The rumor is that the parents' divorce was at least partly attributable to the house.

There was another, even more common, complaint. In the cause of a unified concept, Wright had long been accustomed to designing down to the last detail, and that included the furniture, leaving the individual owners no scope for self-expression. One owner, who loved the house for its beauty but not its constricting atmosphere, felt "spooked" by Wright and thought he was fighting her "every inch of the way." What Wright loved about a new project was the aesthetic challenge, the more intricate the better; practical considerations were sometimes second-ary. When, on the West Coast, he experimented with concrete blocks, hollow concrete shells inlaid with steel, and their refinements, textile blocks, he liked the effect so much that he used it for the Arizona Biltmore Hotel in Phoenix and several private houses in Los Angeles. The results were strikingly original, even monumental, but, again, had a flaw that was not immediately apparent. The curator of the Freeman House in Hollywood, California, said he could "aim a hose at them full tilt all day long and not have a drop of water hit the ground." And one of the drawbacks to Wright's houses that owners often mentioned was the difficulty of hanging pictures on walls that seemed perversely designed not to accommodate them. This antagonism to paintings got him into real trouble when he started designing the Guggenheim Museum.

As I struggled to come to grips with Wright's work, I kept thinking of Berenson's method of training the eye to look and look until one had penetrated into the heart of the matter. The late Adelyn Breeskin, the curator who discovered Romaine Brooks and mounted her exhibition, was once hospitalized flat on her back. I asked her what she did to keep herself amused. "Oh," she said, "I think of my favorite pictures and project them onto the ceiling. Then I look at them." That could never be me, and when, in the middle of my cram course, I went to London, I was unprepared for my reaction. Driving in from Heathrow Airport, I was so dazzled by the multiplicity of styles and fascinating ornamentation that met my eye that I thought I was going blind. Once I had returned to my usual heedless lack of awareness, it was something of a relief. But for a time I had the privilege of looking at the world the way artists and architects routinely must see it. One of the many anecdotes attesting to Wright's visual acuity had to do with cars. Two Lincoln Continentals were lined up side by side in his garage. Wright looked at them for a long time and then decided one of them was three inches higher than the other, and he was right.

London was never high on Wright's list of cities worth saving, and so, during World War II, when it was suggested that he be given the job of rebuilding that horribly bombed metropolis, he gave it about two minutes of thought. Since the motor car had vastly increased the scale of modern life, he recommended that London be rebuilt twenty-five times larger than it was before. Given the size of the British Isles, that argument received the scorn it deserved. Still, the British accorded Wright an admiration that was scarcely returned; in 1941, years ahead of its American counterpart, the Royal Institute of British Architects awarded him a gold medal. Wright, as a loyal Welshman, was intensely opposed to helping the British win the war, so he must have found that a bit embarrassing.

During one of my visits to Spring Green, I stayed at Aldebaran, one of the many farms dotted about the valley that looked toward Taliesin on its dominant hillside. Aldebaran, the name of the brightest star in the Pleiades, also means "follower," and it was once owned by William Wesley "Wes" Peters, a tall, black-haired giant of a man with an antic sense of humor, who showed up at the gate of Taliesin one day and never left. He arrived at an opportune time, as far as Wright was concerned. After the tumultuous decade of the 1920s, when Wright was being hounded by a vindictive second wife, had fallen in love with Olgivanna, had an illegitimate daughter and been thrown in jail, he was, as usual, bankrupt. He had started the Taliesin Fellowship as a way of paying the bills. Peters turned out to be not only a devoted apprentice, but a source of major funding. As heir to a newspaper publishing fortune, he was constantly bailing out the master and at one time bought Taliesin to keep it, as it were, in the family. He was the Fellowship's authority on engineering, but, as an architect, had the Wrightian vocabulary without the master's sensibility. Aldebaran had been drastically remuddled,

Frank Lloyd Wright surrounded by apprentices in the 1930s

at least downstairs, and its forlorn exterior was the only reminder that this had once been an unassuming American farmhouse.

When I arrived on the scene just two years after Olgivanna's death, the Fellowship was regrouping under the benign leadership of Carney, Peters and Brooks. Some of the senior members, like Peters, had been there since the early days, when, as Wright liked to say, they were getting their hands dirty with the mud from which the bricks were made. Some twenty to thirty apprentices, most of them young men, were at work repairing, restoring, remodeling and farming the estate as well; they dug, hoed, planted and harvested. What was not apparent to the visitor was that Taliesin was, as Peters called it, "an architectural sketch." The last time the house burned down, in 1926, Peters said that Wright simply leveled the land, pushed the ashes off the hill and built on the bare soil, which was "not very satisfactory," Peters continued, a diplomatic understatement. "Once I was digging a six-foot trench and dug up a Han horse's head and fragments of Ming roof tiles. I took them to Mr. Wright and he said, 'Wes, finders keepers.' Did I keep them? Sure I did." The house, as flimsy as a stage set, with no storm windows and no insulation, in a climate where the temperature could drop to −30°F, was heated with wood they felled and cut themselves, in roaring steam boilers that had to be constantly watched. Richard Lloyd Jones, a skeptical observer, quipped, "Frank has invented slave labor," which was not far from the truth. But in Wright's defense, these were the Depression years, when just managing to survive was a kind of triumph. And the hard manual labor was of a piece with his belief that architecture took practical training that could not be taught in classrooms. After the war Wright was invited to give lectures at architectural schools for a while. But then the administration found out that he was exhorting students to "go home and make something of themselves," and the invites dried up.

In that transitional period I found longtime fellows and former fellows who were freer to talk about their experiences than, probably, they would have been had either of the Wrights still been alive. One of the most valuable guides was Jack Howe, an architect who had been his chief draftsman and author of many sets of drawings to which Wright would grandly affix his own seal. He was the one who understood Wright's reactions, his strengths and weaknesses; to say he "managed" him is not quite right, but he certainly used enormous tact. He said, "If Mr. Wright wanted something, we had to have it ready yesterday because he couldn't wait. But if his clients were applying pressure, they could wait because, he said, 'I am an artist.' " Howe was chief mediator in the delicate balancing act that was required in order to save Wright from himself. And he shared adventures with an aplomb that would have been impossible for most people. When the Fellowship began its twice-yearly treks between Spring Green and the Arizona desert camp in the 1930s, they used to travel in car caravans with agreed-upon meeting places. One year Wright decided he wanted to go by way of Death Valley and the Grand Canyon, which he had never seen. First they got into a sandstorm in Death Valley and could not move until all the carburetors had been cleaned out. "Then we went onward until we were approaching the north rim of the Grand Canyon. We had no headlights and did not know where we were, but Mr. Wright kept telling us to drive on. Finally he said, 'Better stop here,' and we all pulled up. When we got out we discovered we were fifteen feet away from the edge." What the others thought about being on the verge of disaster is not recorded.

By the time I arrived, Howe and his wife, Lu Sparks Howe, who worked in Masselink's office, had long since left Taliesin, and Olgivanna was the reason why. Everyone credited her with making the Fellowship work—"Wright would have lost his patience and sent us all home in a week," was the general verdict. Over the years she went from standing in the great man's shadow to becoming a personage in her own right. After his death she managed what had become a lucrative architectural practice. That was acceptable, but by degrees Olgivanna came to believe she should be the ultimate authority on artistic matters as well, and required experienced architects like Jack Howe to submit their designs to her. Because her own taste was garish—she liked clashing colors and leopard-skin cushion covers—that was the last straw, and several couples left, including the Howes. Others began to see the formation of what looked like a czarist court. Some couples believed she worked to ruin their marriages, intercepting their letters and filling them with doubts, her purpose being to ensure that their loyalties were to the Fellowship rather than to their families. One of the most telling examples of this kind of malevolent manipulation, as many believed, involved Wes Peters and the wife who became the second Svetlana.

It came about in a curious way. Olgivanna's first marriage, to the Russian Vlademar Hinzenberg, ended in divorce. They had a daughter, Svetlana, who was about twelve years old when she moved to Taliesin with the Wrights. Everyone was charmed by her. She was animated, artistic and mature beyond her years, a skilled hostess and a hard worker. Wes Peters said that she started riding in the truck with him, hauling in the heavy logs to heat Taliesin. "If Mr. Wright and her mother quarreled, she could talk to them and iron it out when she was only fifteen. No one had more understanding of a person's needs than Svet. She shone in every way." He called her "my Svet."

Pretty soon they fell in love, but she was only fifteen and the Wrights were naturally antagonistic. So, in June of 1933, they both left Taliesin. He went back to his parents in southern Indiana and she took lessons from a violinist with the Chicago Symphony. They were married when she was eighteen. All was forgiven and they moved back to Taliesin. Wright, who had adopted Svetlana, was now Wes Peters's father-in-law.

By the time Svetlana was thirty, she and Wes Peters had two sons, Brandoch, aged four, and Daniel, one and a half, and were expecting their third child. One morning in September of 1946, Svetlana was driving a jeep outside Spring Green when the car suddenly swerved, plunging into a shallow stream and overturning in four feet of water. Her children were in the car with her. She and Daniel were killed and Brandoch was thrown clear. No one knew quite how the accident happened. Olgivanna was suicidal, and Wes Peters sank into a depression.

Years passed. Then Svetlana Alliluyeva, Stalin's daughter, defected to the west and published a best-seller, *Twenty Letters to a Friend*. That a member of Stalin's immediate family should flee from communism made for headlines, and there were photographs of her everywhere, along with numerous interviews. At the height of her fame, Olgivanna Wright invited her to visit Taliesin. Svetlana accepted. It was a whirlwind courtship all around. Wes Peters proposed and they were married in the spring of 1970. A daughter, Olga, was born a year later.

I met Svetlana Alliluyeva—now Lana Peters—long after the marriage had ended. Wes Peters was still alive, but Stalin and Olgivanna were both dead. To my surprise, Svetlana was living just outside Spring Green. I made contact with her, she replied with a note and a phone number, and we met. She was, I recall, very attractive, with a wonderful mass of red hair. At one point she was seated on a bench, her feet dangling, and I was struck by how small they were and how out of proportion her head seemed to her diminutive build. She was animated and full of humor, and an initial visit led to several other encounters. Despite her relaxed air, I learned that she was in financially desperate straits and had sent a letter around to friends asking for money. "It is hard for me to beg," she wrote, "but I must continue to write. This is my worst time I have ever met."

She was working as a translator and had written two further autobiographies, but had been unable to find a publisher. She thought perhaps I could help. I offered to try. Bit by bit, she started to talk about her marriage.

Exactly why Wright's widow had invited her to visit Taliesin was never clear. Olgivanna's sympathies were at their most generous when she felt the person had been badly treated. Perhaps she believed that Stalin's daughter would feel at home in what was, after all, another kind of commune. She had never adjusted to the death of her own Svetlana, and now another Russian Svetlana had miraculously appeared. As for her son-in-law, one is reminded of Gala Dalí, who was very matter-of-fact in similar situations. Bettina Bergery said that she once told Gala she had lost her cat, a ginger-and-white male. Gala thought about that, and arrived at Bettina's apartment one day. She was carrying a ginger-and-white cat captured inside her folded-up skirt. She had found it on the street and was offering it as a replacement. One wonders how much this new Svetlana was being presented in the same spirit. What seems amazing is the alacrity with which Wes Peters snapped her up.

With similar backgrounds, the two women were at first on good terms. Svetlana was at first absorbed with her husband's physical problems—he was in his late fifties and subject to debilitating bouts of diverticulitis—and his financial ones. He was deeply in debt, which surprised no one who knew him, since he had no business sense and had bankrupted himself bailing out his master. Svetlana paid off almost $460,000 of these debts; she then advanced a further $300,000 to Brandoch to start him on a cattle-raising venture that subsequently failed. At that stage, Wes still owned Aldebaran, but even when the Taliesin Fellowship was in Spring Green he preferred to stay there rather than at their nearby farm. Given that Svetlana began to complain about Taliesin's demands on her husband's time, the stages by which Olgivanna's euphoria changed to dark and bitter suspicion are not hard to imagine. Svetlana wanted a life of their own outside Taliesin, but, as Wes Peters explained, Taliesin *was* his life. The marriage soon broke up. Svetlana was equally bitter, convinced that she had been invited into the Taliesin circle for her money. "I've been called, asked to pay, thrown out—and forgotten," she wrote.

In the years following her divorce, Svetlana moved between the United States, Britain and Russia, returning frequently to Spring Green. Having experienced the same kind of dislocation, I sympathized, and tried to find a publisher for a biography about her without success. As she was at some level uncomfortably aware, Svetlana was a public figure not for who she was, but for whom she represented. And she very much resented the view of Stalin as a monster. The fault lay with the people around him, she insisted; unfortunately, "Stalin's Daughter Loves Him" does not make headlines.

I knew of her deep concern about her daughter, who seemed to share her mother's sense of being rootless, as well as the burden of the name she carried. Svetlana told me that Olga would often say to her, "Why do I have to be a Stalin? Why can't I be a Peters?" Perhaps this was the allure of Spring Green for Svetlana, who had never stopped loving Wes Peters and nurtured the hope, perhaps, that one day they would get back together again. When she discovered I was staying at Aldebaran, she asked with hesitant formality whether she could visit. She arrived early one evening and went through the rooms without comment. We ended outside on the porch, with its wide views of fields rolling away from the house and the distant silhouette of Taliesin across the valley. She said quietly, "I used to sit on this porch while I was married to Wes and dream of a happy life."

Of all the life histories I have told in my thirty years as a biographer, that of Wright is the most Balzacian in its grandeur and scope. Even if a project began in an unpromising way, I have always managed to end up liking my subjects—life is too short to spend with people one can't stand—but Wright was a special case. There were so many reasons to dislike him: his narcissism, casual exploitiveness, refusal to honor his debts, his selfishness and boastfulness. And yet. One cannot help admiring a man who stands on the burning roof of his house, as he did in 1926 when Taliesin was again ablaze, his hair and eyebrows scorched, defying life to do its worst. He was indomitable. He was also aware of his many shortcomings and, at his best moments, contritely attempting to improve. And he was genuinely funny, an aspect of his personality that does not always transfer onto a page. He was, as the French say, *séduisant, attachant.* At the end, I couldn't bear to have him die, so I made use of a dream Herb Fritz told me to give the final pages the indeterminate ending that I thought the great man deserved. The next thing was to give talks about him, and I gave enough lectures to begin to feel some confidence. Once, at the Smithsonian Institution, I had a standing-room-only crowd, which quite took my breath away.

So I began with a few extemporaneous remarks about trying to sell a book at the bottom of the down escalator at Woodward & Lothrop's, and what a pleasant change this was, though I don't think the audience got the message.

Then I gave the same lecture in London. I had polished my points and honed my jokes, so I accepted an invitation from the Architectural League, about which I knew practically nothing. Naturally I thought this must be a league of architects, but it turned out to be a sort of school with a modest lecture series. I showed up one evening with my slides and found a scattering of adults in the audience and some bored-looking boys in their late teens, perhaps thirty in all. This was disappointing, but I was there to amuse and so I was going to do my best. Unfortunately I had a lot of slides to show, which meant after a bit that the lights had to go down and I had no way to judge the audience's reaction. It was an hour-long lecture, and I knew from experience the anecdotes that had always produced a laugh from my American audiences. But something strange was happening. They didn't laugh at the first joke, or the second, or any of them in fact. When the lights finally went up, I felt as exhausted as an actor trying to explain the humor of P. G. Wodehouse to an audience of Oklahomans. Had I become so Americanized that I no longer knew what my compatriots would find funny? The applause was so subdued you could have dropped a paper clip and it would have sounded like a bullet.

Later that evening the organizers kindly took me to dinner at a very nice restaurant. We had a drink or two and I began to apologize for my poor showing. "Oh no!" they said. "You were fine." "But nobody laughed at my jokes!" "They were smiling," they replied loyally. I was not convinced. Bit by bit the truth began to dawn. The bored-looking boys had a way of dealing with obligatory lectures. They showed up at the beginning, waited until the lights went down and slipped out. "You don't understand," they said. "You were a great success. They didn't leave!"

Chapter Seven

Hidden in Plain Sight

I remember the exact moment when I decided I had to write a life of Leonard Bernstein.

I was on my way back from visiting the late Fritz Gutheim, architectural historian and scholar, who had read my manuscript on Frank Lloyd Wright and was returning it with his comments. He had a house in Dickerson, Maryland, about half an hour away from where my husband and I were then living. It was the morning of October 15, 1990, and Bernstein's death had been announced the evening before. I turned on the radio. They were playing the *Symphonie Fantastique* by Berlioz. I hardly listened at first, having heard it so many times, but then something caught my attention. I was suddenly reminded of the sketch made of the author Charles Dickens when he was at the height of his fame. He sits at a desk, pen poised, and hovering above him are a multitude of scenes and characters that have come from his astonishing imagination. This was happening to the "Scenes from the Life of an Artist," as the symphony is also called. Ribbonlike waves of color, twisting, mingling and re-forming in patterns of almost eidetic intensity, took hold of my inner vision. I almost drove off the road. The orchestra was the New York Philharmonic, and the conductor was Leonard Bernstein.

Deciding on a subject is mostly a cold-blooded business of

Leonard Bernstein, c. 1965

weighing the subject against potential markets, timeliness, the availability of material and the likelihood of getting the story, the kinds of factors publishers have to worry about. In this case my editor, Victoria Wilson, had the same kind of irrational conviction. She said she had dreamed about Bernstein for three nights in a row. We had to do the book, no matter what. And in this particular case I had actually met my subject. Just after my first marriage ended, I was living in an old house outside Georgetown with our three young children, and was living hand-to-mouth as a freelancer for the *Washington Post*. I had begun to get some interviewing assignments, and when Leo Sullivan, then editor of the Sunday arts section, asked if I would like to interview Leonard Bernstein in New York, I jumped at the chance. Bernstein was now principal conductor of the New York Philharmonic and had recently led his first concert in the brand-new Philharmonic Hall at Lincoln Center. He was about to perform in Washington.

There were a few slight drawbacks. In order to get the fifty-dollar freelance fee, I had to turn in a story by the section's Friday-night deadline of 8:00 p.m. However, I could not interview Bernstein until the end of the Friday-afternoon rehearsal, which went until 4:30 p.m. Somehow I had to talk to him, write the article and be ready to start dictating—in the days before e-mail—by 7:00 p.m. It was tight, but there was all that money at the end of it—half my weekly budget. I would do it.

The interview took place in September 1963, two months before the assassination of President Kennedy. That Friday afternoon I was allowed to sit in on the rehearsal, and went up in the elevator with a boisterous crowd of musicians. "Oh, do we have a new secretary?" they asked with friendly leers. I was reminded of Koussevitsky's comment to Bernstein, "My boy, dey are bandits." There was more banter once the conductor arrived. He was certainly good looking, if a bit harassed and already becoming gray, I noted in my youthful arrogance, as well as shorter than I expected. He was a few minutes late and slow getting started, a pattern that would become familiar to me once I started on his biography. The violinist Kenneth Mirkin told me, "I remember one rehearsal [for the New York Philharmonic] in which he came in ten minutes late. Then he had to go around kissing everyone and took out some joke horoscope book and read everyone's horoscopes for forty-five or fifty minutes." At the end of the rehearsal, Bernstein was just hitting his stride. The personnel manager told him his time was up, and "Lenny had a fit."

Having no idea what I was up against, I naturally thought that once the rehearsal was over, an interview would begin. That was when Bernstein treated me to an unwelcome demonstration of his already spectacular ability to procrastinate. As he sat on his stool, one man after another came up to engage him in conversation. Then, like Haydn's *Farewell Symphony*, they packed up and tiptoed out, one by one. Eventually the stage was a forest of empty chairs and music stands, but Bernstein was still sitting on his stool. The stagehands arrived; more hugs and kisses. I finally climbed onto the stage and began to hover. It was 5:30 p.m. and I was about to break out in spots. Bernstein, with a sigh, picked up his score, felt for his cigarettes and suggested we move to his dressing room. I noticed that he was wearing a bright red turtleneck and a gray suit with a silk lining in the same flashy shade of red. At about a quarter to six he sat with a cigarette and a thermos of black coffee and began to talk. Then he talked for the next forty-five minutes.

I don't remember now how I managed to write the story on a borrowed typewriter and meet my deadline. What I do remember is that there was no superfluous conversation. I was used to throwing away the first half hour—when I got to be spoiled, I would ask for three-hour interviews and throw away the first *hour*—but everything he said was quotable. Confessing that he felt out of place as head of a key orchestra in the twilight of symphonic music, he added, "Sometimes I feel a little like a museum curator, hanging out the old pictures for people to see." It was a comment that was picked up by other newspapers and went around the world. He was original, thoughtful, amusing and to the point. That was my first, and last, encounter with Leonard Bernstein. As I came to realize, I had been given a clue to the complex nature of an irresistibly engaging and paradoxical personality.

This one encounter would eventually lead me to a decade-long immersion in New York's intersecting musical and theatrical worlds. However, all I could think about at the time was that I had brought in a windfall. Fifty dollars. We were rich!

The older I get, the more sympathy I have for families who discover that some stranger has decided to write about their famous member without, as it were, so much as a by-your-leave. As Michiko Kakutani observed, too many biographies had become trashy exposés, even those so-called serious studies once thought immune to the gossip-magazine treatment. Prurience titillates, the more the better, leading to bigger sales and better royalties for the writer who is, not to put too fine a point on it, making money from others' misfortunes. There are, of course, exemplary lives, but few of us lack some hidden embarrassment. A secret revealed can, on the one hand, help to humanize the portrait but, on the other, depending on the emphasis, it can also overwhelm a narrative, eclipsing the reason why anyone would want to value such a person. Meanwhile, family members can only exclude—they can hardly prohibit, although some have tried. No wonder they close ranks; they must feel, as John Arbuthnot observed in the eighteenth century, that biography is "one of the new terrors of death."

So I suppose I might have discreetly withdrawn when my letters stating that I had been engaged to write about Leonard Bernstein were greeted less than enthusiastically by his children, Nina, Jamie and Alexander, and his business associates at Amberson, the production company he founded that was headed by Harry Kraut. Six months after signing my own contract I found out that Humphrey Burton, a British television producer, had been hired to write the official life. Bernstein had left an enormous archive—some accounts were that it contained every piece of paper he had ever touched, including canceled airline tickets—that eventually would be given to the Library of Congress. But first the rights to the archive had been sold to Doubleday, Burton was engaged to write the book and everyone else was cut out.

People who write salacious portraits are, of course, the mirror opposites of those who used to write discreet, hagiographic ones; both distort by omission. I have always thought it ought to be possible to write an evenhanded study, using a subject's temperament and experiences to discern the links between life and art. It was not my job to weigh and find wanting on the one hand, or gloss over the truth on the other. Like any playwright, I couldn't tell them, but I could show them and let readers come to their own conclusions. It is rather difficult, however, to establish one's credentials in a new field. One can say with fair confidence that audiences for biographies fall into specialized categories, and people who buy art-related books seldom buy books about musicians and vice versa, as Amazon.com astutely discovered years ago. So, although I had written in the fields of art and architecture, no one in the music world seemed to know or care. If the art world is made up of a hundred pivotal people who all know each other, those who circle around the worlds of classical music are an even more select and impenetrable coterie. True, I knew some people in New York, largely because of Julius Rudel and Ned Rorem, whom I had come to know through my Paris contacts. Then again, as a reporter I had followed the career of Roger L. Stevens, first chairman of the Kennedy Center, and he was an old friend (I thought). My husband knew a wide circle of Washington musicians, composers and conductors. I ought to have been optimistic. But there was the small matter of the official biography. It was the worst of all situations: two biographers in a race to publish first, and I, on the outside, was at a decided disadvantage.

It reminded me of the time some years before when we went to the Walpole Historical Society annual dinner and met a retired druggist. We were then living in this unspoiled, sleepy New Hampshire town and found ourselves seated next to the elderly resident, who had watched local enterprises dwindle and die, including his own. "And what do you do, young feller?" the druggist asked my husband. "I'm a musician and my wife is a writer and we are hoping to get some work around here," he said. There was a silence. Then the druggist said, "Good luck anyway."

Roger Stevens is one of the people who do not get written about, for reasons having nothing to do with his intrinsic interest as a person or with the surprising, Horatio Alger nature of his career. He began work in Ohio during the Depression, pumping gas, then somehow worked his way into buying and selling commercial real estate, for which he had a natural aptitude, being amiable, closemouthed, quick to see an advantage and with a retentive mind for figures. One of his complaints, when I came to know him, was that he had a head full of old telephone numbers. He kept two secretaries working full time, but I never knew him to refer to them or anyone else when called upon to give the latest report on one of his many projects. By the time I knew him he had bought several hotels, including one in Columbus I remembered fondly, having stayed there. His career as a real-estate developer reached its logical culmination when he bought and sold the Empire State Building. That triumph seemed to settle something in his mind, and at moments when he was not fund-raising for the Democratic Party he was indulging in his passion, backing Broadway shows. When he was named first chairman of the National Endowment for the Arts, and then chairman of the Kennedy Center for the Performing Arts, it naturally crossed his mind that he now had another venue for the plays and musicals in which he had invested. I do not believe that the *Washington Post* ever drew anyone's attention to this clear conflict of interest. In any event, Stevens used to joke that he could not be fired from the Kennedy Center because they never paid him anything.

He was in his sixties when I knew him, toweringly tall, usually dressed with great lack of imagination and a natural darling of arts reporters because he unfailingly returned every phone call before the evening deadline. He and his wife, Christine, gave endless dinner parties and I was usually invited. Once, at closing time, Roger quietly suggested we stick around, and pretty soon President Johnson and Vice President Humphrey were ushered into the room. That was Roger, the insider's insider, who always got the best ringside seat and knew all the secrets. He had one forgivable flaw, being partial to expensive wine. More than once, during our tête-à-têtes at some exclusive New York restaurant or other, Roger, in a burst of bibulous feeling, would let slip the kind of high-powered remark that he would not have wanted to see in the next day's paper, and I, silly me, had never printed it. No good deed, they say, goes unpunished. I took Roger out to lunch and told him about my new Bernstein project. "Who's talking to you at Amberson?" he wanted to know. I told him no one. "Well," he said, laughing, "if Harry Kraut won't talk to you, I won't either."

Among the reasons why I wanted to talk to Roger was his early involvement in Bernstein's Broadway career. When it looked as if *West Side Story,* the new musical Bernstein had collaborated on with a book by Arthur Laurents and choreography by Jerome Robbins, was in financial trouble, Stevens provided a bridge loan; pretty soon the up-and-coming producing team of Robert Griffith and Hal Prince took over. I was to hear the tortured start of that famous musical over and over again as I examined it from Bernstein's point of view, then Sondheim's and Prince's, and finally Richard Rodgers's. Later on, Stevens coproduced another Bernstein musical, *1600 Pennsylvania Avenue,* that was a colossal flop. What Stevens allowed himself to say on either subject was minimal and that, for the moment, was that.

If, thanks to Roger Stevens, I received one more lesson in the journalistic maxim that you do not ask a question until you know the answer, in the case of David Diamond I received a human insight into the predicament of the classical music composer. Like Bernstein, Diamond showed marked musical ability and promise, and in his case dedicated his life to the ferociously difficult task of writing for a symphony orchestra. Diamond won endless awards and fellowships and still lived most of his almost ninety years in extreme financial difficulty. He had trained as a violinist, and at one time played in the pits of Bernstein's musicals by night and worked as a clerk at a soda counter by day. Like Bernstein, he made it his business to know everyone who mattered. Also like Bernstein, he had a certain edge over confirmed heterosexuals at a time when the casting couch for aspiring young composers and conductors was horizontal. People told me that David Diamond used to wear makeup, but when I met him he looked like a quintessential professor of music, dressing conservatively and walking through the Juilliard School of Music with a quick, self-important step. Still, if money was his measure of success, he had failed. As Noel Annan wrote, "To succeed, painters and writers had to become celebrities, and celebrity destroyed them as artists."

Diamond was widely read and, happily for my book, eager to talk. I spent a weekend in Rochester, New York, where he lived in the kind of American suburb that scarcely exists anymore, accessible by public transportation and close to a small, lively shopping center with actual sidewalk cafés. To my surprise, it was the house he had grown up in, and although it was a bright, sunny day, all the blinds were drawn. He was living in a twilight of his own making, and some people who knew and liked him nevertheless believed he was a fantasist. I was never sure. He had spent several years in Florence and could well, as he said, have known Romaine Brooks and Natalie Barney. The fact that he had read my obscure book was naturally one of the first things I liked about him. On the other hand he had little to say about them, Sir Harold Acton, Bernard Berenson or others of the world I knew so well. As we spent hours talking, I began to see that his relationship with Bernstein was nuanced and complex. Naturally enough, although Bernstein had given big performances of his Symphony No. 5 and Piano Concerto, Diamond was always nudging Bernstein to do more and exploiting the sense of mission and guilt that Bernstein felt for contemporary composers less fortunate than himself. Their correspondence shows that Bernstein regularly sent him money, even remembered his birthday, would lecture him about his health and once, according to Diamond, saved him from suicide. I began to wonder whether Bernstein could ever have done enough to satisfy Diamond. I also began to see what an enormous advantage prominent conductors like Bernstein had, since performances of their own works were guaranteed. Diamond was resourceful but Bernstein, that ace diplomat and manipulator of the music business, was cleverer.

The rise of the Mafia presumably came about as the result of social chaos; this could well be true of the music world. Too many people were clawing for a foothold, and a few unscrupulous men and women at the top were making or breaking careers with impunity. So it was that Dimitri Mitropoulos, a confirmed seducer of boys, got Lenny into bed and incidentally became his chief enthusiast. So it was that Arthur Judson, who dominated the music world as Bernstein was entering it, functioned as an independent concert agent and also manager of the New York Philharmonic. This double role was a clear conflict of interest, but, like Stevens, he was never challenged. Patrick Hayes of the Washington Performing Arts Society said that when Judson asked you to jump, you asked, "How high?" So it was that promising young musicians startled like frightened fawns when I appeared on their horizons. During one visit to Tanglewood I surprised one of them at a public pay phone as he called New York, presumably to Amberson, asking, "This Meryle Secrest. Is she legit?" The same thing happened with others, like Michael Torke, a young composer, who responded enthusiastically at first and then, some days later, was only willing to mumble a few generalities.

On the other hand, members of the in crowd, no longer in favor, were happy to fill me in on what they saw as nefarious dealings. These, paradoxically, did not help either, because they did not want their names used and so I had no way of documenting their assertions. Ever since Alan Clark, I had been on the alert for informants who might be likely to make revelations they would later disown, leaving me to take the consequences. This continued to happen periodically. One prominent figure in the music world told me a scandalous story that would certainly have made for a lurid trial in the London libel courts. He was most disappointed not to find the anecdote in my book. I noticed, when he subsequently wrote a memoir, that he did not publish it either. This made my chapter on Amberson's business dealings less useful than it might have been. Fortunately, Norman Lebrecht, then music critic for the London *Daily Telegraph,* had much more to say in his own book, *The Maestro Myth,* and said it better. Well, you can't expect to be liked in my business, but with any luck you can avoid going to jail.

Through David, I met another Diamond. She was Irene, a fascinating figure who had begun her career in Hollywood when she was working for Warner Brothers and discovered the play on which *Casablanca* was based. She met Bernstein through Marc Blitzstein in the early 1940s and was very much impressed with him. "He was young, very beautiful and tremendously alive. He had all sorts of interests and a total passion and commitment to music." When she learned of a plan to make a movie about Liszt, she suggested Bernstein and he went to Hollywood to make a screen test. "He was star-struck," she said. "I have to say he wasn't bad—he was so articulate, he couldn't be bad at anything." He wasn't great, either, and the idea was dropped.

At the time we met, Irene Diamond was heading a foundation in memory of her late husband, a successful real-estate developer, that was financing worthwhile pilot programs in medicine, education and much else. Before she died, she had the novel idea of spending the fund's capital until nothing was left, which she successfully did. The foundation had its headquarters in a discreet suite of New York offices; hers was naturally the largest. I was ushered into a handsome paneled study with a heavy desk at the far end, behind which sat a tiny person with an unruly halo of white hair. She was wearing a black dress with the daintiest little Peter Pan white lace collar. I didn't believe that white lace collar for a minute. After I got to know her I realized I was right; behind the deceptive demeanor was a sharp, commanding personality. She took charge of me right away. Robert Redford, she said, was a friend. She happened to know he had always wanted to play the role of Frank Lloyd Wright. How would I like to sell my book? For a split second I measured my memory of Redford, whom I had seen walking the corridors of the *Washington Post* when he was making *All the President's Men,* against my inner image of Wright. They did not match. Oh well. "I suppose you've written a screenplay before?" she asked carelessly. As a matter of fact, I hadn't. Never mind; I would learn. I allowed myself to float through the next few days buoyed up by the alluring possibility that my biography of Wright would sell to the movies. Then I had another lesson, this time about Hollywood, by way of Irene Diamond. When we next met for lunch, the Wright idea was off. It was not going to work because, after the murder and arson of 1914, everything else would be an anticlimax. It was perfectly amazing how fast one could be picked up and dropped. On the other hand I somehow knew it was for the best. I would never make a screenwriter.

I met so many unforgettable personalities through my investigations into Bernstein's life. There was Mary Rodgers, daughter of Richard, who had worked on his television programs for children; Alison Ames, U.S. director of Deutsche Grammophon, his eventual record producer; there was Peter Mark Schifter, who would direct Bernstein's last opera, *A Quiet Place;* Johanna Fiedler, daughter of Arthur, late conductor of the Boston Pops; Richard Bales, his contemporary and future director of the National Gallery Orchestra; Kiki Speyer, whom he almost married; the composer William Bolcom; Tim Page, future Pulitzer Prize–winning music critic of the *Washington Post;* Evelyn Saile; Stefan Lorant, founder of the British *Picture Post;* and so many others. There was also Arthur Laurents, the playwright for *West Side Story* as well as *The Time of the Cuckoo*, starring Shirley Booth, a play I had seen on Broadway and passionately admired. I felt honored to be in the presence of a great man of the theatre, one who turned out to have my own voracious interest in human behavior along with a stunning ability as a raconteur. Through Arthur, I at last had the details I was looking for about the personalities, evolution and ultimate success of Bernstein's best-known musical. The sales of my biography were disappointing, but praise from a few people who knew him well made up for everything. Among them was Arthur Laurents. He wrote, "I marveled constantly at how you made points without either hammering the individuals or softening the facts." He said, "You got it exactly right."

When I went in search of Stephen Sondheim, another of the pivotal figures of *West Side Story*, I knew that he was the reigning genius of the Broadway musical. As a young composer, Sondheim was brought in to give wit and point to Bernstein's labored lyrics. He went on to collaborate with Arthur Laurents on *Gypsy*, then to write his first full Broadway score, *A Funny Thing Happened on the Way to the Forum*, and to begin his long and successful collaboration with Hal Prince on *Company, Follies, Pacific Overtures, Sweeney Todd* and *A Little Night Music*. As happens with the kind of quick characterizations favored by newspapers and magazines, the view of Sondheim had fossilized into caricature. It was said he was brilliant but strangely reclusive, eccentric and taciturn. He wore a beard and tattered sweaters. The impression was that he lived in Bohemian squalor.

So when he agreed to talk to me about Bernstein, I was apprehensive. Late one afternoon I visited his five-story, nineteenth-century row house in the fashionable Turtle Bay district, where he had lived and worked for three decades. The traffic noise outside was deafening; inside, the lights were low and the atmosphere hushed. Just entering that space gave me my first

Stephen Sondheim, 1950s

surprise. The living room was furnished with comfortable sofas in forest greens, beiges and duns, and decorated with Sondheim's rare collection of antique toys. Tables cleverly positioned under spotlights held impeccable potted plants, in this case a poinsettia, giving a splash of color and adding to the sense of restrained and elegant stylishness. The dining room behind was full of tropical plants in huge pots, and one could just catch a glimpse of that rarest of all luxuries in New York, a hidden garden. Discreet noises came from the kitchen, where Luiz Andrea Loureiro, Sondheim's majordomo, worked culinary miracles. This was the kind of establishment where one was served coffee in a Limoges cup, tiny black stripes on a white ground edged with gold. So much for Bohemia.

In a way I was not surprised. In my youth I had worked in the public relations department of F. & R. Lazarus & Co., department store, which was then playing a leading role in the cultural life of Columbus, Ohio, by means of its imaginative display windows, taking their themes from museum exhibitions and theatrical productions, and its lectures, films and special events. Its exclusive Wedgwood Room showed designer creations; I particularly liked the dresses, suits and coats made by Herbert Sondheim. I used to wander up there to admire the designer's latest creations: beautifully cut, expensive clothes in enchanting color combinations, that looked dashing but not outré and, unlike some of the wares on display, were always flattering to the figure. It was not much of a surprise to find that Stephen Sondheim's father had founded a Seventh Avenue dress house and that his mother was a fashion designer.

My second discovery was how easy Sondheim was to talk to. To call him taciturn was a joke; all you had to do was propose a question and he was off and running. In the course of our conversation he suggested that Bernstein's late, disappointing works, such as *A Quiet Place,* had failed because he was trying too hard to make a statement. Bernstein had a bad case of "important-itis," he said succinctly. That seemed exactly right and became a major theme for the second half of my book. Sondheim may have told me then that he had written a board game, The Great Conductor, in which aspiring music students try to track down the elusive Bernstein. He is an unpredictable moving target across continents, protected by secretaries, agents, blocked phone calls and locked dressing rooms. It sounded full of fun and I told him so. "Listen," he said. "That's what I should have done." He told me about another game, Hidden in Plain Sight, in which the challenge was to find an object hidden in full view, but camouflaged so successfully that it was almost invisible. The playwright Anthony Shaffer liked the idea so much that he made finding the hidden object the life-or-death search of one of the characters in his play *Sleuth.* The play won a Tony award in 1970 and was later made into a film starring Laurence Olivier and Michael Caine. The more I thought about it, the more con-

Sondheim's father Herbert, the dress designer, 1956

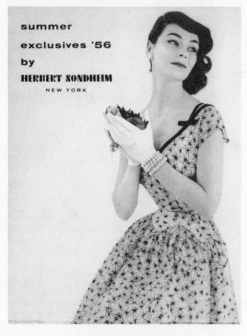

summer
exclusives '56
by
HERBERT SONDHEIM
NEW YORK

One of Herbert Sondheim's creations

"A bad case of important-itis": Sondheim with
Leonard Bernstein, celebrating *West Side Story*

vinced I became that a biography of Sondheim would be a fascinating project if the composer would sit still long enough for a
portrait.

So I sent him a letter: thanks, but no thanks. I waited a year
and tried again. That was the year my biography of Bernstein
was appearing. Sondheim was polite and friendly, but still said
no. That was also the year Arthur read the book and gave it his
enthusiastic thumbs-up. He relayed his enthusiasm to Sondheim; "Don't be surprised if he says yes," he wrote. Shaffer's play
had briefly been given the title *Who's Afraid of Stephen Sondheim?* I won't say I was afraid, but I knew better than to ask
myself my usual flippant question, "How hard can it be?"

In the fall of 1994 I paid a second visit to Turtle Bay. I had
wondered how to bring up the subject, but Sondheim began

right away by saying he did not mind if I talked to his friends, but hesitated about being interviewed himself because it would take too much time. It sounded as if the book's central character would be out of focus, and that would not do at all. I launched into a description of Romaine's childhood and the parallels I saw between her life story and my own. When I got to the part about Romaine having had the worst mother, he stopped me. "No, *I* had the worst mother," he said with a laugh. I then talked about my own feelings and years of self-examination and must have shed a tear or two. He *had* to let me write about him, I said. As I spoke, he looked kinder and kinder. Little did I know the effect such a display would have on him, and seeing anyone in distress was absolutely the one thing he could not bear. Without quite knowing what I was doing, I had won his cooperation.

That was a major turning point in my career as a biographer, and that late afternoon in October was one I would never forget. I took note of everything: the tiny iron railing between the house and the street, the creaking gate, the leaning flower boxes full of impatiens, the brass nameplate and the same impression of almost womblike retreat, an Aladdin's cave. I had not fully appreciated the way the narrow entry led into a high-ceilinged space with curving walls and curving staircase, the shades of brown, the colors of tobacco, the sets of rare playing cards mounted on the walls, and all those charmingly archaic board games behind glass cabinets. I was greeted by Steve Clar, Sondheim's young, slim secretary, a small elderly dog and a large, friendly black poodle called Max.

I was offered a vodka and tonic—"We have everything"— and Sondheim seemed to be drinking straight vodka in what could have been shot glasses; he replenished his glass from bottles in the freezer. He sat back against the sofa with one arm along the back, wearing rumpled pants and a bluish-green sweater, the left sleeve of which was twisted around his arm, something he did not seem to notice. Because he spoke so rapidly, I realized I would have to forgo my usual practice of taking shorthand notes and use a tape recorder; the whole point of the exercise would be to get verbatim quotes. I was somewhat unprepared for his reaction when I sat down in a chair beside him. He immediately leaped up and moved to the far end of the sofa. I was too close; well, I was used to European reserve and emotionally distant people. When he spoke he never looked in my direction, but talked, as it were, into the air. I somehow knew that this, too, was a self-protective measure that would fade over time. Arthur Laurents once remarked, "You ooze sympathy." Was that bad? "Not at all," he replied. "There isn't enough of that in our world."

Sondheim said he would get a list of friends from Steve Clar, and it turned out to be a long list. He made a couple of spontaneous suggestions about things he would show me, including a unique game he had found, and his latest computers. He had persuaded Arthur to buy one, and was going to convert *me.* He had a private phone number at his Connecticut house that he would give me "eventually." He then began talking about a time frame and confided that he had begun work on a new musical for the Kennedy Center's twenty-fifth anniversary in 1996, and swore me to secrecy about it. It was to be based on Alva Johnston's book *The Legendary Mizners,* about a colorful pair of brothers. One of them was Wilson Mizner, a Broadway playwright Johnston described as "fundamentally a confidence man whom circumstances occasionally induced to go straight." Mizner also made the immortal remark, during the Fatty Arbuckle scandal, that living in Hollywood was "like floating down a sewer in a glass-bottomed boat." As for Addison Mizner, he was a self-taught architect who designed houses for the wealthy in Palm Beach and Boca Raton. Sondheim said, "Just as when you look at me you feel like crying" (not quite right, but never mind), "when I think about the ending of Addison's life, *I* feel like crying." Apparently, just before he died, Addison Mizner had succeeded in persuading the city of Boca Raton to build a ten-lane highway to connect it with Florida's network of interstate roads. It went for half a mile and ended in a dirt path; it became a road to nowhere. As I left, Sondheim leaned forward from some distance away to shake my hand. Then he said, "The floodgates are open."

In a way it was mad to go back to the idea of working with the cooperation of someone who was still alive, as I had done with Kenneth Clark. On the other hand, Sondheim was not encumbered with a hostile son, or indeed any children at all. I had the idea I could build the book around his own comments, let him tell the story in his own way. Almost none of the reviewers realized I had used the structure of the infinitely extended interview. Not very original, but safer. Everything, of course, depended on my success as an interviewer, and I have to say we got off to a rocky start.

Almost as soon as we began talking, Sondheim said that the playwright John Guare had come up with an anagram of my name: Merely Secrets. (I was grateful at least that my name had not provided the building blocks, as had Salvador Dalí's, for something like Avida Dollars.) Sondheim seemed to imply this was a sinister omen, and I could have wrung Guare's neck for planting a seed of distrust, knowing that allaying my subject's suspicions would take every ounce of diplomacy I had. What made me think I could do it? Why would Sondheim allow me, as an Englishwoman, an admitted outsider in his world, no musician, not a New Yorker or with any of the other reference points he might have looked for, into his life? Why not someone young, male and bright-minded, fresh out of Juilliard, who could also write? How could I hope to keep up with this subtle, rigorous, quicksilver personality, let alone understand him? How could I avoid unknowingly making a faux pas that would make him even more distrustful of his decision? That, of course, is immediately what I did.

In 1995 Steve invited me to a reading of a murder mystery he and George Furth, his collaborator on *Company*, had written. No music; it was a straightforward comedy-thriller, then titled *The Sins of the Fathers,* set in a psychiatrist's waiting room. I had attended theatre readings before without protests from the management, and was unprepared for the litany of complaints I received the next time we met. I sat in the front row, taking notes. That put the cast off their stride. I ought to have been in the back, trying not to scare the horses. I had smiled at him; that was wrong, too, and I remembered he had fixed me with a terrifying grin. I had laughed out loud; that was another faux pas. I should keep my voice down in restaurants because people knew his name. Since I was pretty confident we had not been to a restaurant together yet, I asked him for an example, and he dropped it. He had not asked me to keep the plot a secret, so I told Mary Rodgers about it and that somehow got back to him. He was angry about that, too. I seem to remember she claimed the plot was her idea, which may have been why Steve was so miffed.

I realized later the minefield that rehearsals and previews represent for anyone trying to launch a new production. Sondheim and James Lapine, author of the book, faced enormous hurdles when they were preparing *Passion,* their uncommercial story about a hopelessly plain woman whose love for a handsome young soldier becomes an obsession. When it opened in 1994, John Lahr, theatre critic for *The New Yorker,* called it "Love in Gloom." The drama coincided with the arrival in Sondheim's life of Peter Jones, a poetically handsome young composer, and in January 1994 they had exchanged wedding rings. More than professional pride was bound up in that musical, and the previews had been excruciating. The audiences were not just armchair critics who went in order to dislike the work, or assistants to rival producers, or press agents whose job it was to put out the bad word, but ordinary theatregoers, many of them tourists, who are the biggest ticket buyers in New York nowadays. These audiences could not believe what they saw as a completely farcical plot. The authors identified twenty places in the musical where disbelieving laughter was being heard in the wrong places. It was as if Sondheim, who, for the first time in many years, had fallen in love, made a public statement of his emotions; now rotten eggs were being thrown at him from the balcony. No wonder Sondheim was so on edge about behavior that would seem to him as intrusive or inappropriate. As he said later, in another context, about critics, "it gave them the chance to shoot me through the heart . . ."

For some reason Sondheim had not thrown me out, so I followed the fortunes of *The Sins of the Fathers,* which became *The Doctor Is Out* and, once it arrived in New York, *Getting Away with Murder.* More work was needed. Sondheim and Furth were taking their fledgling to San Diego's Globe Theatre, where, as nurtured into shape by Jack O'Brien, and evolving through its West Coast premiere, it would presumably emerge sturdy enough to survive whatever barrage of criticism lay in wait. It was agreed I could go to San Diego.

Even when one is sitting in front of a rehearsal, it is almost impossible to figure out what is happening. Actors stop and start. People run in and out, sit down and stand up. They fluff their lines. The director, O'Brien, makes a joke you don't get. The curtain rises and falls, stopping three inches short of the floor, displaying a small forest of ankles. This must all have some dreamlike significance, if only one could figure out what it was. Meanwhile, Sondheim and O'Brien are in constant consultation and one does not dare try to read lips. George Furth is on the sidelines. What is going on, I ask. He says, "You're a writer and I don't talk to writers." The problem is not me, but him, he adds; if he says anything at all, he will be in trouble.

There was no particular significance to the fact that the curtain would not go all the way to the floor; it was just the faulty mechanism. Jack O'Brien is sitting across from me, wearing khakis and a long-sleeved shirt and eating a sandwich. Without his horn-rimmed glasses he has an impish, puckish, Noël Coward look. His manner is unruffled; he seems almost offhand. "I have just realized we don't use the front of the stage. It would help so, so much." He wants all the furniture brought forward six inches. It sounds absurdly arbitrary, but, as it turns out, he is right.

Sondheim is running up and down the aisles to talk to the actors, fingers fluttering. Or he sits slumped, feet dangling over the backs of chairs, wearing his usual muddy browns and looking heavier-eyed than usual. "If you see me looking like this," he says, "it's because I've had *too much* sleep." But I notice he yawns and rubs his eyes. It is the morning following a $500-per-ticket black-tie dinner in his honor, and he was the only one not wearing formal clothes. His father used to insist he dress for the occasion, which is why "I'm a slob." That night there was a run-through, an act of "almost cruel folly," according to O'Brien. I ask Sondheim how it went. "Okay," he says. I look at him inquiringly. "Well, you know how these things are."

The play is set in a psychiatrist's offices in a derelict building somewhere in New York. The murdered doctor's body is in the next room, but the group-therapy patients who arrive do not know this. There are seven, each representing one of the deadly sins; the psychiatrist personifies the eighth (because he's playing God). Much of the action requires split-second timing and precisely controlled shifts of mood. "The dialogue has to be funny until the moment when it isn't," Sondheim explains. "If we are one inch off, they will laugh all the way through" a scene that is meant to be creepy. So there are cuts, rewrites and constant changes in blocking going on this morning. O'Brien says, "We've done a nearly complete rewrite of the first act in one day." Will it answer the objectives? "We'll see," he says cautiously. Steve is boasting about his six new sentences. "Your six Aristotelian sentences," O'Brien says. "Please teach George how to do that." I venture that by the time I get hold of a copy of the script, the whole play will have been rewritten. "Oh dear God," O'Brien says. The actors are desperately trying to recall all the changes in blocking, dialogue, intonation and bits of business. The whole process of putting a play together seems to have a lot in common with group therapy: people with big problems and common goals, defending each other and hoping it will all work out in the end. And occasionally collapsing with laughter. The murderer, played by John Rubinstein, has invented a new bit of business. He dispatches each victim with the comment "Let me solve the problem for you."

"What I wanted to do," Sondheim said, "was have a play in which you would discover the murderer at the end of act one, and the second act would be 'How does he get out of it?' So the first act's Agatha Christie and the second act's *Dial M for Murder.*" He made reference to *The Last of Sheila,* a murder mystery film he had written with Tony Perkins in 1973 that became a cult classic. *The Doctor Is Out,* as it was now being called, was a logical outcome of his interest in the form, and there were aspects about the play that made O'Brien think it, too, ought to have been a film. "There's something—boy's work about this," Sondheim added, which was what he had also said about *The Last of Sheila.* "It's because it's moving things around. It's fun. But it *is* game-playing."

At the Sunday matinee the play was well received, although the audience did not get the point about the eighth deadly sin. This was supposed to have been clear from a taped confession by the psychiatrist himself, but was being drowned out by background noises. I mentioned this to O'Brien, who said he knew, and that it would take him the rest of the week to get the play so that the audience *did* hear it. I was invited to sit in on the postmortem in the greenroom, and to my surprise, as notes were being given to the actors, Steve slid next to me. He explained that the differing audience responses from Saturday night to Sunday afternoon had to do with the actors' growing mastery of the material. There was a buzz of optimism in the room, and Steve leaned toward me: "There's the sound of a happy cast." The loudest laugh came when O'Brien said he would like the cast, at the moment when one of the group talks about his lame leg and useless left arm for the umpteenth time, to groan. O'Brien's imagination was even more bloodthirsty than his own, Sondheim said. O'Brien made some other comment during the note-taking and I, forgetting myself, said, "I agree." Sondheim hushed me, but he was smiling.

On opening night in March 1996, my husband and I were supposed to have been asked to the cast party but never received any invitations. In fact, we did not know there was a cast party. When we went to Joe Allen's afterwards, we were surprised to find Jack O'Brien there with a group of friends, having dinner. As soon as the curtain descended for acts one and two, Steve was nowhere to be found. This was, perhaps, his usual method of operation. On the other hand, I suppose I should have picked up the signs and portents, which seemed clear enough to everyone else. Clive Barnes's review in the *New York Post* received the headline STICK WITH THE DAY JOB, STEPHEN. By letting the audience know who the murderer was at the end of the first act, most reviewers seemed to think that the authors had sacrificed suspense. As for the second act, Broadway audiences did not like the fact that the serial killer did, indeed, get away with murder. The villain's fate was quickly changed so that he, too, met the end all right-thinking theatregoers expected. But by then it was too late. The play cost $1.5 million and closed in a week. Final advertisements showed a gargoyle holding a gun to its temple with the caption "Goodbye, cruel world."

One of the first times we talked, Sondheim was lying comfortably on a couch, and toward the end a tape recorder fell out of his pocket. It reminded me of the time when Maître Emanuel slid each page of a letter across a shining surface and then waited while I copied it. He soon gave up that idea and I assumed that, since I was also taping, Sondheim would eventually trust me to get it right. To that end I recorded every "um" and "ah" of our two-hour sessions, something like fifty hours of tapes in all, transcribing them myself so that if there were mistakes in the transcripts, I alone was responsible. Having such a complete record turned out to be an advantage when the time came to get his permission to use the quotes. When he asked, "Did I say that?" I could show him the passage, and to his credit he never claimed to have been misquoted. The interviewing process is routinely described as adversarial and criticized if it is not, to which I would say, that depends. It is true the interviewer has to keep a certain distance from the emotional field in the interests of getting the story, choosing the moment carefully when it is safe to ask the subject, for instance, about his or her love life. I had not yet found that moment.

I also believe certain questions should never be approached in the larger cause of not revealing what your subject has a right to keep to himself, or of not holding him up to public ridicule. It seems to me that to invite someone's confidences and then betray that person is a kind of treachery. Sondheim's mother had made sexual advances to him, had lied to him and wished he had never been born; he had been betrayed enough. However, knowing what not to ask is so difficult to measure and such a fine line to cross that, in the last analysis, everything depends on trust, and that goes two ways. If Sondheim was beginning to trust me, I also was beginning to trust him. It happened at the moment a kind of teasing exchange began. One evening in February 1995, I had a phone call from him. Something truly terrible had happened. There had been an electrical fire in the house, and by the time an alarm was sounded it was well advanced. Luiz Andrea Loureiro had to be rescued from his fifth-floor apartment with a ladder, and Max, the poodle, had died of smoke inhalation. The house, with its wonderful decor, its furnishings and precious objets, was mostly destroyed. Given all this, I could not quite account for Sondheim's energized, almost playful tone. "This is all your fault," he told me. "It is?" I replied. "This had better be good." It turned out that some extension cords in the office had been hidden beneath the carpeting. I had asked for photographs, and these had been brought out of storage and unwittingly placed on the carpet on top of the extension cords. It was only a matter of time before the wiring became hot enough to burst into flame. Then a toilet on the second floor flooded and put paid to whatever had not already been damaged by fire. It was going to take two years to put the house back together again; meanwhile, Sondheim needed to find an apartment for himself and Peter and some way to go on working. Shortly after that, I found myself calling him by my husband's name. He caught it fast.

"Wait a minute, wait a minute."

"I mean Steve," I said.

"I like that Freudian slip," he said.

"You'll never let me get over that!"

He replied quietly, "No, I'll just remember it."

While he was, for the moment, otherwise engaged, I was doing interviews in New York. I learned that he had been in love with Lee Remick, actress and film star, who had taken a leading role in one of his early shows, *Anyone Can Whistle.* So once in a while I would ask his friends about that relationship. No one was being particularly indiscreet, but those who had seen them together thought it was a real romance. One evening I went out to dinner with a friend who had watched the relationship develop, and we had a long talk. Shortly after that, Steve reproached me for having discussed his private affairs. He said, "You're getting dangerously Kitty Kelley here. Very Kitty Kelley," he said. So I suggested he tell me about Lee Remick, and he began talking about her in low tones with long pauses, and was

Lee Remick with, from left, Arthur Laurents,
Stephen Sondheim, and Harvey Evans, 1964

slurring his words. It was obviously very difficult for him to say anything, and I noticed an unconscious gesture: he kept taking off Peter Jones's wedding ring and putting it back on again. This reluctance carried over to everything else we discussed that day. He was in an impatient mood, wanting to be done with it, or me. So I cut the session short after an hour.

However, I was due to return the next day and realized that there was more to be said. My notes of June 1, 1995, record what followed:

Spent a lot of time thinking about what happened yes-terday as I wasn't to see SS until noon. So I decided to write a "speech" to make sure I said it in the right way. Wrote s.thing to my satisfaction & then thot some more (in Saks). Decided that the only way to do this was to be prepared to back off & do the book on my own—But it was as much to his advantage to keep me corralled as my own, & this helped. What really bothered me was the idea of my every move being relayed back to him. When I went in he pretty quickly saw that something was up—he said, "You look upset," so I tried to adhere to my little speech but threw it away quickly as I got teary. (I said I would overlook the reference to Kitty Kelley as I was sure he did not mean it and had the satisfaction of seeing him look shamefaced.) I said I was hurt that he would think me capable of a prurient book.

But then he immediately said he hadn't meant that at all, & he trusted me implicitly. Then I said I couldn't be double-guessed all the time, & he said that he merely objected to my talking about Lee Remick before I had talked to *him*. Then he tried to continue the argument about what my informant had said, & I stepped in & told him he must have heard this at third hand because my informant told me he had not spoken to SS for months. This seemed to be the case. I'd say it was a draw. He still seems to think he can "call" me on things but I don't see any evidence that he wants to back out, whereas I realize I am prepared to do that if necessary.

Oh yes—he said something about writing a biography being a "love affair" for two years, or three, or however long it took. Not my idea, I must say.

I was late for my next appointment, because he really held on to me & started giving me a bunch of London phone numbers (eleven!) just as I was leaving. So naturally I took them—he's so careful about giving out numbers. He was the one who brought up seeing each other in London next month—I didn't. Am not sure I want to see him in July. He likes scenes & reconciliations, & I don't. They upset me & make him feel warmer. As I left he was all smiles & patted me on the back. I don't like this—he's too sharp & cold for me but I suppose I can understand his suspiciousness. I have learned from this, however, that I must express my feelings & stop him—otherwise his accusations get wilder & wilder if not challenged.

All day yesterday & this morning I was driven mad by a persistent irritating itch on my left cheek. Something between a tickle & a jumping muscle. This morning as well. It's gone now!

N.B. He showed me a present he'd just rec'd from Steve Clar, rescued from the fire, its left upper edge charred, but otherwise unharmed. It is a sheet music copy of the song he wrote for *Follies,* called "I'm Still Here."

When the finished copy of the book arrived, I spent a few minutes admiring it. Then it suddenly occurred to me that if I had a copy, the books were being shipped to the stores then and there. I could imagine the following phone call to Steve from a friend: "Steve, I've just seen your biography at Barnes and Noble." Reply: "Well, *I* haven't seen it yet." Something had to be done. I must personally deliver what was, for the moment, my only copy, suitably inscribed. Steve Clar suggested I come to New York the next day, when Sondheim was in a recording session with Patti LuPone. We could meet there.

It was about noon when I arrived at the studio, and as luck would have it, Steve was coming down the stairs, accompanied by a friend whose name I did not catch. They were going to have a drink and suggested I join them. We sat at the bar. I was on Steve's left and his friend was on his right. We ordered drinks and I took out my package and slid it across to him. "There's your book," I said. He, to his friend, "Oh it's *my* book today? It was hers yesterday. She must have had a bad review." He turned it over, examining it this way and that, and I was reminded of Elaine Stritch's comment that when Sondheim really liked something, no one was ever as pleased or complimentary. "I even like the binding!" he said.

There were so many reviews that for the first and last time I put them all in a ring binder. Most of them were pretty good. The only reviewer who was critical of my refusal to open the bedroom door was Patricia Holt, book editor for the *San Francisco Chronicle,* who said I had not "nudged or probed" Sondheim, and that he had "few intimacies to discuss." Most reviewers seemed grateful that I had not written a tell-all book; perhaps the market was drying up at last. Steve had read the book in manuscript and corrected a number of errors. After he'd finished reading it, he called and said, "I had to read it all the way through to find out whether I died." That was typical of his humor. I was sure he could not have liked some of my conclusions, but he did not challenge them; he respected my opinion. Since gratuitous comments by me were precisely what Kenneth Clark and his family had not liked, I had good reason to be grateful.

I went on a lengthy book tour. I think the day in San Francisco was the most demanding; I counted seven interviews, including a couple of TV appearances, which although short, are surprisingly tiring. At the end of the day I was pretty well exhausted and there was still another date, at Brentano's, where I was to autograph books. I had learned to dread those sessions. It was almost always a case of the author surrounded by piles of books that nobody wants to buy, and that evening was no exception. I was seated to one side of the front door and noticed that a motorcycle had pulled up outside. An exceedingly tall man wearing blue jeans and jacket, festooned with chains, a red bandanna on his head and a beard going down to his waistline had descended and was coming into the store. There were a couple of clerks about, and that was it. I thought, Oh dear God. I saw him walking in the opposite direction, to the sales counter, and I breathed more easily. But then, horror of all horrors, he was making a beeline straight for me. He was clutching a copy of my book. Finally he loomed over me and started to speak. In a Mickey Mouse squeak, he said, "Would you please . . . ?"

On author tours from city to city, one is usually picked up by a guide whose business it is to get visiting writers wherever they are going and then wait around for them. One was usually met by a lady driving a red VW Bug, only slightly rusty, and the back seat was either full of dog or battered copies of *Be Here Now* and *Zen and the Art of Motorcycle Maintenance.* Or maybe she was breeding hairless cats; at any rate, your guide was always friendly and efficient and would tell you how much she would like to write if only she could spare the time.

But when I arrived in Los Angeles, I was met at the airport by a chauffeur wearing a double-breasted gray uniform trimmed with brass buttons and a cap to match, and escorted to my car. Not just any car but an enormous stretch limousine, the kind where you are seated so far back that the driver, as Dave Barry would say, is in another county. And it was pink. I felt everyone staring as I was deposited in my pink leather seat surrounded by telephones, and introduced to my copies of *Variety* and *Entertainment Weekly,* my bottles of Evian and my handy refrigerator full of Dom Pérignon. Something was definitely wrong here.

The chauffeur and I chatted for a while, then he asked, "Are you a film star?"

"Oh no," I said hastily. "I'm just a writer."

In the days when I was working at the bank and trying to find a reporting job in Hamilton, Ontario, it seemed logical to earn some money singing in a nightclub. This was not as quixotic an idea as it sounded. I already had some experience with a dance band in Bath, thanks to my uncle Don, who played saxophone at the Pavilion on weekends. It was almost routine. I sang the songs I knew. People bobbed about beneath me doing the fox-trot and the quickstep and nobody paid any attention; they certainly did not applaud. I had no way of knowing, at the age of eighteen, that the nightclub scene in the United States was, notoriously, run by the mob, and probably in Canada as well.

I went to see a talent scout who turned out to be a middle-aged, paunchy man in a fedora. He was sitting at an almost empty desk in a small green room and thoughtfully chewing tobacco. He looked me up and down for a while and then softly recommended me for a tryout. I hoped there would just be one as I only had one decent dress. I somehow assumed there would be an orchestra and I would sing in the background, comfortably ignored. Instead, one evening I was ushered onto what became a series of minute stages lit so blindingly that I did not know who was in the audience, if anyone. Then I was left to my fate. I would sing a couple of songs and be summarily evicted into a grimy corridor. Kitty Carlisle Hart, who began her career singing in New York nightclubs, told me years later that she'd never had any trouble with her mobster employers. You were either a good girl or a bad girl, and she was judged to be the former. Heaven knows what they thought of me; since I was barely out of a gymslip they probably did not think of me at all. For my farewell appearance, I managed to leave the heel of one of my shoes behind on the stage. I was too embarrassed to go back for it.

I had an ear for music, so I sang the songs I heard on the radio, like "Blue Room," "With a Song in My Heart," "There's a Small Hotel," and "If They Asked Me, I Could Write a Book" (my signature tune). In my ignorance, I had no way of knowing that I had gravitated to the songs of Rodgers and Hammerstein and particularly Rodgers and Hart. Even after I met Mary Rodgers and confessed that one of my favorite pieces was her

Richard Rodgers, 1950s

father's "Slaughter on Tenth Avenue," it still had not occurred to me that there might be a biographical opportunity there. Rodgers had written an autobiography, Hugh Fordin had written a biography of Oscar Hammerstein, and Frederick Nolan, a biography of Lorenz Hart. There was a Rodgers centennial coming up in 2002, and there was the Bernstein book.

I received the shock of my life one day to get a letter from Mary Rodgers. She loved the Bernstein book and wanted me to "do one on Daddy." By then I was certainly on my guard about needing a family's cooperation. She and her sister, Linda, had a sizable family between them and, in addition, there was the organization set up by Rodgers and Hammerstein during their lifetimes to protect their commercial interests. This meant lawyers not far in the background, as I knew. On the other hand, there was the lure of the subject itself, the chance to revisit the triumphs of *Oklahoma, Carousel, South Pacific, The King and I* and *The Sound of Music,* the possibilities of unearthing some new material and the chance to work with Mary. I remember a lunch at the Rodgers and Hammerstein offices at which the family's control over the manuscript was the central issue. Would the book be authorized or not? The question hung in the air. I was getting ready to stand up and leave if the family wanted manuscript approval. My hands were on the arms of the chair. Then Mary Rodgers said slowly, "No . . ." I should have stopped then; I didn't believe them.

Mary was a figure in her own right. Like Linda, who became a gifted pianist, Mary excelled in music and arrived on Broadway in 1959 with a star, Carol Burnett, and a musical of her own, *Once Upon a Mattress.* She wrote scores for *Hot Spot,* starring Judy Holliday, *The Mad Show,* and *Working;* then a best-selling children's book, *Freaky Friday,* which became a Disney film. When I knew her she was chairman of the board of the Juilliard School and much else, happily married to Hank Guettel, the mother of five grown children and mistress of a spacious Central Park West apartment, decorated with exquisite taste.

Before I met Mary Rodgers, mutual friends told me I would like her immediately, and they were right. The British used to talk about "side"; she had none. She was down-to-earth, approachable, an interviewer's dream, since she always had something original to say, and quite frank. She had a charming way of not only introducing a new friend into her circle but embracing that friend without reservation, something I, with my remnants of English formality, found disarming. During the war Richard and Dorothy Rodgers had taken in Zoë d'Erlanger, the daughter of mutual friends in London, whose mother was killed in the Blitz. Zoë stayed with them throughout the war and ever after was referred to by Mary as "my English sister."

This kind of instant acceptance permeated the offices at Rodgers and Hammerstein on Broadway. I dealt mostly with Theodore S. Chapin, president and executive director, and Bert Fink, director of public relations, who presided over the work of

Mary Rodgers with her father, excelling in music

protecting Rodgers and Hammerstein's artistic oeuvre. There were always new productions of the shows to be carefully monitored, there were copyright issues on the songs and casting decisions, all of which needed Rodgers and Hammerstein approval. The staff struck me as perfectly realistic in their attitudes toward the kitschy view of life expressed in the musicals, which were written half a century earlier for a much more sentimental taste; they were clear-minded about the works' strengths and limitations. My first surprise was to find that their newsletter was called *Happy Talk*.

There were other warning signs. I had not appreciated the extent to which Rodgers and Hammerstein now regarded me as part of their big, happy family, an adopted relative as it were. So when I was addressed by one of their secretaries, someone I had never met, by my first name, I objected, in my perfectly proper European way. The girl in question was most offended. This had never happened in her twelve years with the company, she said. I was subsequently told off by Mary, while Ted Chapin listened silently. Did I not understand that I was being paid a compliment, she scolded.

Henry James's novel *The Aspern Papers* is based on an actual historical incident. It seems that Captain Silsbee, a Boston art critic and devotee of Shelley, discovered that a mistress of Byron's, Claire Clairmont, was living in obscurity in Florence, with a middle-aged niece as her companion. Captain Silsbee decided that, since Claire Clairmont was the half sister of Mary Shelley, as well as the mother of Byron's illegitimate daughter, she might well possess some valuable papers. On a pretext, he talked his way into their household, rented a room and hung about hopefully. After a while the old lady obligingly died and he put the question to the niece. The niece had, indeed, inherited valuable papers. She was perfectly willing to let him see them provided that he became a relative. In fact, he must marry her. He fled.

In the coming months I thought a lot about *The Aspern Papers*. I was so used to being on the outside that I was unprepared to find myself being drawn into the family dynamic. In fairness, members of the Rodgers family probably did not know this was happening, either; it was based upon unconscious expectations. It is assumed that the biographer's goals in writing about his or her subject have become synonymous with the family's own. The biographer has agreed to marry them, literally or figuratively, as in *The Aspern Papers,* and the stage is being set for the moment of mutual disillusion.

My predicament at the time became clear enough. As Henry James wrote, I would receive a "just punishment for that most fatal of human follies . . . not having known when to stop." Quite right, too. As it was, I got out my tape recorder and began asking questions. There was nothing I wanted to know that Mary would not tell me. When I was working on my Sondheim project, she had described in detail how she had fallen in love with him when she was only fourteen and would have married him, even knowing that he was a homosexual; how they had decided to get engaged informally, and how that idea had collapsed during a party. Occasionally the person being interviewed has to be saved from herself; as she began to reminisce with almost stream-of-consciousness frankness, I realized she was one of them. What I had not realized was that she was as bitter about her mother as Sondheim had been about his. When she and her husband sent Sondheim a birthday present one year, he replied with one of his quick and devastating one-liners, thanking them for the platter but asking, where was his mother's head. Mary showed a similar antagonism. Before she died, Dorothy Rodgers had several close calls that Mary described as her "annual dying act." For once the problem was not seeing the shadows, but seeing too many shadows, and the picture that began to emerge of Richard Rodgers was not much better. Here was an undeniable genius. He was kind, generous and funny, but he had phobias, was addicted to alcohol and nicotine, had breakdowns, was an incorrigible womanizer and was, most of the time, emotionally unavailable.

The question that bedeviled me was the huge gulf that separated Rodgers's work, particularly after he fell under the ominous saccharine spell of Oscar Hammerstein, from the miserable reality. This psychic split had to have its austere origins somewhere, yet his early letters gave no clues and his autobiography was unrevealing. His daughters had given up trying to understand him; "I don't think anyone really knew who he was," Mary Rodgers said. "I don't think *he* knew. He was just all locked up in there." If the links between the life and the work, the ones I had come to believe were inevitable, were hidden in plain sight, I had not found them.

So I stumbled onward, gathering evidence and waiting for the contradictions to resolve themselves. As I knew from writing about Bernstein, early success brings problems of its own, along with the understandable inner demand to top oneself. On the

Her "annual dying act": Dorothy Rodgers
with Dick, mid-1960s

other hand, as I learned from Bernstein and Sondheim, musical theatre is a form of mental torture. I love the Larry Gelbart quote, "If Hitler is alive and well, I hope he is on the road with a musical." Along with the uncertainties and crises and the catastrophe of failure, Rodgers had to contend with gangsters. He said as much: "When I started [Broadway] was crooked, opportunistic, sordid and sharpshooting." He added, "I've seen it at its worst."

There was a direct connection to the world of laundered money, threats and extortion through "Doc" Bender, Lorenz Hart's so-called manager, whom everyone knew had links with the mob. Exactly how Rodgers might have become enmeshed,

I did not know. I must have made too good a guess. An old Broadway hand, replying to my question, said, "If you quote me, I won't kill you but I'll get you killed. I won't do it myself but I've good connections. One day they will find you somewhere with your manuscript." The quiet, almost laconic nature of the threat was chilling. I recalled that, when I was investigating the art market frauds of Salvador Dalí, his manager, Robert Descharnes, had finessed some awkward questions with the comment, "It's too easy to put a gun in a man's hand for three thousand dollars." That was the moment when I really should have stopped.

As it was, I kept on working and met my deadline with a biography that would be published to coincide with the Rodgers centennial; predictably, the family was not pleased. I was back with the old conundrum I had faced with the Clarks: the private truth versus the public façade, appearance versus reality, the theme that had fascinated me ever since I read *The Quest for Corvo*. After a difficult search I decided that the only title that made sense was *Somewhere for Me,* a quote from the song Rodgers wrote for *No Strings,* his first musical after Hammerstein died. This struck the family as too somber. Mary wanted *The Sweetest Sounds.*

Chapter Eight

The Radstock Hill

During my career as a biographer over the last thirty years, I have often wondered whether any of this would have happened, had I not needed to climb the Radstock Hill. After working at the *Hamilton News* for two years, I took a year's leave of absence to go back to Bath. I was prepared to get engaged to Steve, my grammar-school boyfriend, who was then reading geology at university, and with whom I thought I was madly in love. But two years apart had changed both of us; we scarcely recognized each other. So there I was in England, it was autumn, I had no money and no prospects and was desperate for work.

I spent that Christmas delivering the mail. By the time I heard about it, all the easy post-office jobs were gone, and actual mail delivery, in which you walked around with a heavy sack on your back, was all that was left. Actually it is quite difficult to deliver the mail, even when the front doors are as close together as they were in the row houses just off the Bear Flat in Bath. It is even harder when one is, as usual, caught in a shower and, feeling completely stupid, keeps going in and out of the same gate because you have forgotten to deliver something. Pretty soon I sensed that my lack of progress was being followed up and down the avenues by unseen pairs of eyes from behind lace curtains.

That had its compensations. When they saw that the person lugging the sack was not the usual adolescent boy but an obviously muddled girl, the door would open just as I got to it. A kind voice would invite me inside for a cup of tea, and then another and another. By the time I got back to the sorting office, I was usually desperate for the ladies' room. And a bedraggled mess. But I had a check for five pounds at the end of the week and it seemed a fortune.

By then I was working as a stringer for the Bristol *Evening World,* and had been given Radstock as my very own preserve. I had been hired by the editor of that morning tabloid in the antediluvian days when women were discouraged from covering hard news. He wanted to know why he should hire me, because he would not be able to send me to fires, accidents and murders. I was ready for him. I cleverly said that maybe I could do things boys could not. I had the role of a sob sister in mind. He thought for a moment and then, with an air of kindness, offered me work. It was not, as I had hoped, full-time. It was not even in my hometown. It was Radstock, or what passed for coal country in that part of the world. I would get 1½d, or three halfpence a line for each article they printed. It seemed a pitiable sum, but I was desperate.

To get to the unremarkable little town of Radstock from Bath, you head south, taking the main Wells Road. There is a steep climb to the Bear Flat, where I was delivering mail in avenues named for Tennyson and Milton, reflecting Victorian earnestness of purpose. This is the "Flat" Rowlandson had in mind when he drew pictures of ladies in Empire dresses hanging on for dear life to their bonnets and shawls while the wind, that all-pervasive wind, did its best to blow them off Beechen Cliff.

From there, one faces another steep climb up Wellsway to Odd Down, with the vale of Lyncombe on one's left and Ralph

Bath's Bear Flat, and hanging on for dear life:
from Rowlandson's *Comforts of Bath,* 1798

Allen park somewhere on the right. Then you are speeding across the meandering countryside on the old Fosse Way—those Romans knew a thing or two about the shortest distance between two points—with the Wansdyke and Fortnight Farm on your left and Duncorn Hill and Withyditch on your right, over the Great Western Railway tracks, and on to Dunkerton, Peasedown St. John and on to Radstock.

It is only ten miles, but this is following World War II, there are no new cars to buy, and one has been catapulted back to the eighteenth century, that is, when time was measured by the distance four men could carry a sedan chair, or the endurance of a horse. Now it is measured by how far one can go on a bicycle. And I am about to start work, but have no way to get anywhere except by bicycle. This is a creaky old one I have borrowed from Aunty Gwen's lodger. I am rather surprised, actually, that she has stooped so low as to rent a room to a window washer, but he turns out to be a decent sort. I accept the loan gracefully, even though I have a devil of a time getting on and off his bike in my skirts. The ten-mile trip will take an hour; it ends with a crazy, careening plunge down the two-mile Radstock Hill into the valley below. It goes without saying that it is two miles back up and, in the way of three-speed bikes, there is no way you can ride; you have to walk. It goes without saying that I am hardly looking forward to the trip.

The land over which I traveled was part of the old Kingdom of Wessex. King Arthur, it was said, had won a decisive victory over the Danes at Ethendune in 878 and commemorated that victory by carving a white horse on the Wiltshire Downs. As a child I had skipped along the edges of the Westbury White Horse, just as I had clambered over the ruined walls of King Arthur's Tintagel, now so beaten and battered by water and wind that, to my child's eye, it was only a heap of indecipherable stones. I scrambled up the steep slopes of Cheddar Gorge, the caves of which, I now know, contain skeletons thousands of years old. For years I attended services in the Bath Abbey, site of the crowning of King Edgar, the first English king, a thousand years before. I shivered in the winds blowing through Stonehenge and surveyed the empty plains around Salisbury and danced all night beside ancient Roman baths. And it was over these Wiltshire hills, with their ditches, tumuli, earthworks, intrenchments and barrows, their picturesque names like Dane's Bottom and White Sheet Downs, that my grandfather, Albert Doman, would walk to court my grandmother. It was seven miles from Mere, where he lived, to Maiden Bradley, where she lived, and to make sure he would not get lost on his return in the dark, my grandfather would drop a trail of white pebbles.

Bits of flint, battered coins, broken walls, roads that ran like arrows over the landscape: these were all parts of my world, and they gave me an awareness of being rooted that has never left me. In that chain of intricate associations, Radstock was a minor link. Two of my parents' friends, who can be seen smiling shyly in their wedding pictures, lived in Radstock. Reg James was a miner with the Pensford Colliery, and his wife, Nell, small and

Lansdown Place East after the bombs fell
on Bath in 1942

dark-haired, wearing rimless glasses, had the trim, precise look
of a schoolmarm. Even now the benevolence of their natures
illuminates these blurred photographs. After the Germans
bombed Bath for two nights in April 1942, Nell and Reg took us
in. I never heard the sirens at night and was sound asleep when
my father shook me awake. In my befuddled state, I was trying
to get out of the bedroom door, but there seemed to be something heavy and black in the way. My father found me at the
landing window, trying to climb out. He rushed me downstairs
and into the back garden. Our house, on the hills south of the
city, had a panoramic view of dozens of planes diving on the city,
dropping bombs.

I was too fascinated by the roaring sounds and shooting lights to move and stood as if transfixed. The whole scene was lit up by clusters of flares, interspersed with sudden explosions of flame. It was a theatrical extravaganza being staged just for us, but then why was my father shouting so angrily and pulling me across the grass? Somehow we reached the dubious safety of a neighbor's homemade shelter. We were lucky that night. We only lost doors and windows; in the valley below, hundreds of people died. There is something about the aftermath that is unforgettable; the dust, the acrid smells of burning, the crunch of glass under your feet and the look on people's faces, a kind of blind bewilderment.

By the time I met them again, Reg James had been taken out of the mines because of an accident—he had burned his hair leaning over an oil lamp—and was driving a locomotive. Perhaps it was through him that I wrote the only story of any consequence to come out of Radstock: one about a miner who, after a freak accident, went back to work and died two or three days later. Whatever the *Evening World* did print was usually condensed to a paragraph, which seems to have earned me something like two shillings and threepence, at a time when the weekly average wage was about five pounds. The most money I made on a single article was nineteen shillings and sixpence, almost a pound. I achieved this feat by covering a West of England flower show. Mere words could be cut to ribbons, but the paper, I discovered, would print the name of every single winner, and the list went on and on. It was the easiest quid I ever made. Then I was summoned for an interview by the rival, and larger, Bristol *Evening Post,* and was hired. A full-time job and real money, at last.

"So we beat on, boats against the current, borne back ceaselessly into the past," F. Scott Fitzgerald wrote. The life of a young journalist then was so removed from today's realities that it almost seems as if I dreamt it. In the first place, the apprenticeship system was still in place. It made sense when one considered that my grandfather began work when he was twelve, and my father at fourteen. School-leaving age had become sixteen when I came along, the age at which one's five-year apprenticeship as a journalist could begin. The pay scale went entirely by age, which struck me as very unfair. I was living on four pounds ten a week and soon found myself counting pennies obsessively. Nor was I prepared for the situation I found in the offices of the *Evening Post.* At least at the *Hamilton News,* pitifully equipped as it was, I had been given my own battered Royal. This was a big evening paper and there was not a typewriter to be found. I take that back. There was one, owned by one of the senior reporters. He brought it to work every day, and each evening he carefully locked it up in its case and took it home.

No, you composed in pencil on small slips of paper that gave you room for a single paragraph. You detached the carbon and yelled "Copy!" This was one of the few joys of the system. Nowadays, copy girls and boys sit around at telephones and yawn at each other. In those days, just like the ball boys at Wimbledon, they sprang to their feet and dashed to your desk, then raced toward a small door in the back. After a while I gathered up my courage and opened the door. There, looking as if they had not had a decent meal since 1945, sat six or seven exhausted copy editors wearing green eyeshades. Their job was to read your handwriting, keep track of the running story, and make some sort of sense of it before it ended up on the printed page.

There were several reasons for this curious system. To begin with, newsprint was still rationed and papers had, at most, twelve pages. The only way to deal with the daily drumbeat of news was to have multiple editions. I forget the actual number at the *Post,* but it must have been twelve or fifteen, and there was no connection between the front page, which hit the streets at nine-thirty or ten in the morning, and the late editions at five-thirty or six in the afternoon. Keeping some kind of control over stories that could come and go in a matter of minutes was among the duties of this lonely band of men in their airless room. As for the reporters, you could write a story, have it published and, unless you were quick, never see it. There was great competition for the centerfold, because it ran through all editions.

I was amazingly naïve. I knew nothing about police work or the judicial system, yet I was being sent to cover inquests and court cases, even if these were limited to drunk-and-disorderly and "giving her occupation as actress," presumably idiot-proof. The job was made to order for someone like Keith, who, at the age of twenty-four, was making double my salary, to my annoyance. He was a whiz at shorthand, knew detectives by their first names, coached me on the rules of evidence and was always buying me a beer. Sometimes we covered a story together. Another rather nice feature of the system was that reporters were sent around in limousines (to make sure they got there). You were usually given thirty minutes to cover a story before being driven to another, and if you were wise, you would have everything written by the time you got back to the office. Not that there was much to write. The stories were naturally terse, if not telegraphic, and the deadpan delivery I acquired took years to shake off.

An only child, I had gone everywhere around Bath alone, and it had never occurred to me to be frightened. But to be walking around Bristol just then was an unnerving experience. A bombed-out city, as we saw from the postwar wave of films coming from Italy and France, was not just a city of obliterated buildings; it symbolized the desolation that characterized life in much of postwar Europe. The war had been won, but food was still rationed, clothes were still rationed, there was nothing to buy, and even if there had been, no money to buy it with. The local authorities were bankrupt, and if they did rebuild, they put up nasty little prefabricated houses that were almost worse than the rubble-strewn, wind-haunted streets. Such daily reminders of the randomness of violence had their effect, and I developed a morbid fear of being mugged. This was particularly true at night, when I had a long walk from the bus stop to my lodgings. I went up and down those wet, deserted streets, made even more ominous by the fog lights, which shed a sickly yellow cast over the lampposts and curtained front parlors. I was listening for the footsteps signaling that someone was following me. I developed a technique for looking into windows for the reflection of someone who stopped when I stopped, walked when I walked. I was on my way to a full-blown panic attack one evening when, as I was making a call from a phone booth, I became aware that a man was watching me. What did he want? Obviously he was lying in wait. He was going to follow me and attack me. Whatever was I to do? My only hope was to stay in the comparative safety of the lighted box and hope someone else would come along. I stayed and stayed; he stayed and stayed. Finally I noticed him looking at his watch, and the truth dawned. I came out and he, with a single exasperated glare, rushed inside.

During that year in England, gaining what Peter Jennings called "the free education of life," borrowing that window washer's bicycle propelled me in a life-changing direction. Nowadays, when I begin writing other people's lives, I am on the alert for similar pivotal moments. For Frank Lloyd Wright, life was turned upside down and changed forever the day he left his wife for Mamah Borthwick Cheney. For the young Stephen Sondheim, determined to be a composer, everything changed when he reluctantly agreed to help Bernstein hone some lyrics for *West Side Story*. Richard Rodgers almost became a salesman of baby clothes, Romaine Brooks almost starved in Rome, and if Berenson had not found Isabella Stewart Gardner, or perhaps it was the other way around, he might have ended up doing all kinds of other things, but the odds are good he would not have become an expert on the Italian Renaissance.

Sondheim was right: writing a biography really is a sort of love affair. I fell in love with almost all of my subjects, sometimes at a rather advanced stage, as when I saw the vulnerable man behind Dalí's calculated façade. I fell in love with B.B., even though I knew this was a man one would never want to cross. That special quality of delight in the natural world, that easy transition from the poetry of landscape painting to the evidence of his eyes and back again, the generosity, humor, and insights—how could anyone resist him? I followed him blindly through thickets of theory I even now shudder to recall. I even tried reading the books he had recommended in his *One Year's Reading for Fun*—Heine's *Romantische Schule,* Butler's *Erewhon,* Burckhardt, Nietzsche, Plato, and Goethe—so much for *fun.* My slavish discipleship took its toll on my marriage. The moment I learned anything else about B.B., I would rush into my husband's study. "Darling!" I said, bursting through the door one day, "I've just discovered that Berenson never took his bar mitzvah." He looked at me so patiently, but something made me realize that I'd gone too far. And of course he had to live with Dalí, Bernstein, Wright, and all the others at equally tiresome length during breakfast, lunch, and dinner. In the end, charm of personality is in the eye of the beholder and pretty difficult to convey, which accounts, in the Kenneth Clark case in particular, for a certain flatness of tone in my writing. There seemed to be no way to convey the unique joy he gave others.

My mind is full of images, moments to take out and revisit at leisure on a slow afternoon. I think of Ron Cocking's blank stare at the top of the stairs, that abstracted look that was as close as he ever got to disapproval. On the other hand, his explosive laugh, rubbing his hands and shaking his legs, made the endless revisions he demanded seem almost worthwhile. How many times have we leaned over a table together, as his fingers slithered over scraps of sentences that he had cut down and ruthlessly rearranged, in the goal of teaching me logical sequence? How many times have I despaired of deciphering inserts (A) (Ci) and (X4) and all those other scribbled instructions? The advice he gave me—"dream it up" and "jazz it up"—well, Frank Lloyd Wright always said that firsthand experience was the only way to learn.

I've read that biographers instinctively choose subjects that answer some unvoiced need. Mine was clear enough: I wanted to see worlds and meet minds that otherwise would have been closed to me, and if I was looking for teachers, I could not have been luckier in Berenson and Clark. I learned from Sondheim, as well—that quality of spontaneity and buoyant refusal to be defeated by life that the world of the theatre tests more cruelly, perhaps, than any other art. I often think of the time when Bernstein and I finally got to talk and how much I valued the stimulus of that brief exchange. I think of Taliesin, not the camp outside Phoenix, but the gentle, grave and beautiful house on the hill that is slowly decaying, Wright's enchanted valley and something mystical and wizardlike about his spirit that is unique to my experience. I even like his impossible qualities, from a safe distance, of course, and his sense of man in harmony with the natural world that is rare in any age.

I've learned from everyone and I suppose, in the final analysis, that makes writing biographies a completely selfish enterprise. When ambition comes to an end, something of real value is left, as Berenson always believed: the joy of discovery for its own sake. "With a free, onward impulse . . ." I often think of him revisiting places in Italy where, as a young man, in the remote villages of the Marches, there might be nothing to eat but bread, onions, and anchovies, but where he "tasted the freshness of a spring or autumn morning in a Bergamesque valley as if it were a deliciously invigorating draught." He went to Ravenna where, decades before, the sound of his solitary footsteps had set up echoes. He returned to Venice, that magical world he ought to have painted himself, and which brought him back to his first loves, the Giorgionesque Venetians. He wrote about these journeys in his last book, *The Passionate Sightseer,* and was correcting proofs when he died.

Sometime soon I will take a bicycle back up the Radstock Hill. I don't look forward to the climb but, on the other hand, the next adventure could be just around the bend.

Index

Index

Index

Index

Index

A NOTE ON THE TYPE

This book was set in Adobe Garamond. Designed for the Adobe Corporation by Robert Slimbach, the fonts are based on types first cut by Claude Garamond (c. 1480–1561). Garamond was a pupil of Geoffroy Tory and is believed to have followed the Venetian models, although he introduced a number of important differences, and it is to him that we owe the letter we now know as "old style." He gave to his letters a certain elegance and feeling of movement that won their creator an immediate reputation and the patronage of Francis I of France.

Composed by North Market Street Graphics,
Lancaster, Pennsylvania
Printed and bound by R. R. Donnelley & Sons,
Harrisonburg, Virginia
Designed by Virginia Tan